Alpa[
Alpacas Farming
Alpacas Farming guide to care, diet, breeding, health and costs.

By

Lucy Glasten

Table of Contents

Introduction

I want to thank you for purchasing this book. This book contains proven steps and strategies on everything you need to know in order to successfully raise these beautiful creatures. It's filled with advice and tips that will help you to create a successful relationship with the alpaca as well as learn to use this knowledge to starting your own business doing something you will love!

Many people think that raising alpacas is boring and hard, but that's not true! You can easily raise alpacas and it does not require much effort and time to raise them. Raising Alpacas is certainly one of the best decisions you can make. It involves understanding their nature, and also taking into account that the choice of raising Alpacas can be a life changing experience. The success of your love affair with the alpaca breed starts from the moment your alpacas are chosen, so care should always be taken to start the experience off on the right note. This will include understanding where to source your alpacas and what you need to avoid. This book contains everything you need to start your experience of caring for your alpacas from day one, even if you never raised or cared for one. It will guide you every step of the way as you love and care for new alpacas.

This book will also help you to take into account health aspects from dietary needs and the necessary supplements to give your alpaca a very healthy lifestyle. A great read for both homesteaders and potential alpaca farmers alike!

Chapter 1. What You Should Know Before Starting an Alpaca Business

The business of alpaca rearing is perhaps the best opportunity in livestock farming. Alpacas are an appreciating asset meaning that, just like real estate, their value keeps going up. The value of alpacas is so high that even in tough economic times they still remain high in demand. A case study was done in the last economic downturn when demand for all produce was low. The alpacas on the other hand were able to maintain high prices. This is because of the high quality fiber they produce that is always hotly sought after by designers of high end garments in fashion capitals of the world like Paris, Milan, Tokyo and New York.

There are a couple of reasons that make the breeding of alpacas as a business particularly attractive. One of them is the ease of transportation. Compared to other livestock, alpacas are quite easy to transport from where they are reared to market locations. In addition, they have a relatively long lifespan. This means that they are likely to give you monetary returns for a very long time. The fact that they don't often fall sick also means that they are unlikely to cost too much in maintenance. Lastly, the IRS treats alpaca rearing as any other business in livestock. As such, the IRS gives you tax incentives and other financial advantages as part of their bid to encourage investment in the livestock industry.

While, in the last century, there were many people who made big money in livestock, in modern days, there are few examples of people who have made millions from livestock businesses. The business of alpacas certainly won't make you a millionaire but it will definitely give you a handsome income. Apart from the healthy profits it guarantees, it also gives you a chance to live a rewarding lifestyle. It is therefore a worthy business venture to try out if you are keen on increasing your income substantially.

In spite of its profitability, breeding Alpacas is a relatively new business in the Western world. For a long time, it was only limited to Latin America particularly Bolivia and Peru. Export of alpacas was banned as there were fears that their numbers might reduce substantially. In 1984, however, all this changed. Both Bolivia and Peru allowed part of their substantial alpaca herds to be exported. Most of the western world including the US, Australia, Canada, New Zealand and a large number of European countries removed restrictions on the importation of alpacas. More recently, other countries like South Africa and Japan have also begun active importation of alpaca herds. The net result of all this has been a massive increase in the market of alpaca. Since there is not enough supply to meet demand, alpacas have become very costly. This has made alpaca rearing very profitable for farmers.

Chapter 2. Getting Started in the Alpaca Business

It is quite easy to get started in the alpaca business. The first thing to do when starting an alpaca breeding business is to buy a female alpaca. The number of bred female alpacas you can buy depends on the amount of funds available. The good thing is that if there are not enough funds available, you can even start with just one bred female and still grow a lucrative business.

However, before you buy one you need to consider a number of factors as examined below:

▪ Alpacas are very social animals. They can barely tolerate a lonely environment. It is therefore important that, to start with, you buy two alpacas. In case you don't have enough to buy two then you can buy a cheaper and younger alpaca male or request the dealer to give you one. It is not advisable to have other animals as the alpaca's company. Having a horse or goat to provide an alpaca with company will not stop making it feel lonely.

Alpacas have been found to only feel happy when in the company of other alpacas. In addition, having other animals to provide it with company is not particularly healthy for the alpacas. This is because they can easily contract illnesses from the other animals, spread through parasites and other disease causing organisms.

▪ Cheap alpaca are not the best. There is always the possibility that they might not produce a high value offspring. This will substantially reduce your returns. While it is certainly desirable to get an alpaca at a bargain price, it is important that you also take into consideration the quality of the alpaca.

The price range for high quality Huacaya alpaca is, on average, between (£4000) $5,000 or. The qualities to look into of an alpaca before buying are physical strength, fleece, and bite, mothering instincts, color genetics and reproductive health. A quality alpaca should have a high measure of all these.

• Apart from the bred female alpaca, it is also crucial that you carefully examine the quality of the stud from which the female alpaca is bred. The reason for this is that the quality of the unborn alpaca is just as important as the bred female alpaca. This is because it is the baby alpaca that will form the basis of your breeding stock in the future. It is therefore important that you ensure its quality is as high as possible. Knowing the quality or pedigree of the stud will give you a rough idea of the likely quality of the yet-to-be-born alpaca, also called cria. In order to know the quality of the male alpaca or the herd sire, you may start by asking for its photos. With the photos, it's possible to see the visible qualities of the herd sire. These include physical size and strength among other qualities.

This is, however, not enough. You can go further by asking for pictures of some of the alpaca that it has produced. In that way, you will get a more meaningful picture of the quality of alpaca it is able to produce. In addition, you may need to find out the type of ribbons either the herd sire or its offspring have won in shows. Getting this information will greatly help you not only in knowing the quality of the alpaca but also in marketing the offspring of the alpaca in future sales.

• Ensure the person you are buying the alpaca from provides follow up services and guarantees. These should be clearly specified in the sales contract. Of particular importance is the guarantee of 'live birth," if investing on an alpaca which has not yet been born. If you buy your alpaca in the breeding industries you are certainly going to be given this guarantee since it is standard there. However, if the alpaca is bought in an auction you are unlikely to get this guarantee. This is because most of the auctions have no such traditions. The importance of this particular guarantee lies in the fact that it is not always a guarantee that your female alpaca will produce a live offspring. There is a possibility that things might not go as expected.

The alpaca might have a re-absorption or a miscarriage. When this happens, you will have met the costs of breeding again. This is very expensive. Having a guarantee of live birth in your sales contract will cover you against such unfortunate incidences. This is because you will be offered free re-breeding. In addition, find out if there are any other services that the alpaca breeder offers for free as well.

• In choosing a female alpaca, go for the older ones. The older alpacas, in most cases, would have either one or more offspring unlike younger, maiden alpacas. Even though these younger alpacas look more beautiful, it is hard to know their fertility level. If, on the other hand, you buy an older alpaca, you will be sure that it is fertile. In addition, the fact that it will

10

have already produced a cria means that it will not be problematic in producing another one but also nursing it. This is because it already has the experience. The maiden alpacas, on the other hand, have no such experience. They are therefore likely to have difficulties producing a baby alpaca as well as taking care of it.

If, however, only maiden alpaca are on sale it is important that you first of all check the records of not only her dam but also the reproductive records of the female members of her bloodline. In doing so, you will be able to have a rough idea on her fertility levels. When buying an alpaca, always remember that the focus is not on the alpaca you are buying but rather the potential offspring of that alpaca.

• Be careful to get genetic diversity when buying an alpaca for rearing. This is very critical since it gives the offspring hybrid vigor. Related alpaca usually have related qualities and therefore the offspring usually lack hybrid vigor. In order to avoid this, try as much as possible to buy the alpaca as far away from your neighborhood as possible. By doing so, you greatly reduce the chance that the alpaca bought might be related to the alpaca already on your farm or in the neighborhood. As such, when it reaches time for re-breeding her, you can comfortably use the male alpaca in the neighborhood without fearing that they might be related.

However, this does not mean that you should avoid entirely buying from the neighborhood. Buying from the neighborhood creates goodwill as well, ensuring that in case you need a breeder in the future, you will easily get one. In addition, it also helps you establish crucial business contacts. In the alpaca breeding industry such contacts are very valuable since they offer some valuable information which is the key to your success in the industry.

In order to balance the need for hybrid vigor and the advantages that come with buying locally, you can decide to buy some alpacas locally but breed them far away when that time is reached and then also buy some from far away but breed them locally. In that way you will be able to reap the benefits of getting the best of both worlds.

• In choosing the mode of transportation of the alpaca, choose a safe and comfortable one. This is particularly important when you are transporting the alpaca for long distances. Transporting alpacas in uncomfortable vehicles for long distances usually has a negative effect on their health. They are likely to lose weight and suffer from diarrhea. In addition, they are also likely to be lethargic and show signs of pain. When buying alpacas from a far off place, it is therefore important that you use a mode of transportation that is going keep them comfortable during the whole journey. In most cases, those who sell the alpacas have comfortable vans that can be used

- To transport the alpacas allow for those needs. Not all businesses, however, have such facilities. That is why it is important that when hiring a van to transport them, you choose a van that will give them comfort. The best van is one with air conditioning. Alternatively ask the dealer selling you the alpaca to recommend the most suitable transportation facilities around.

- It should, however, be noted that not all alpacas are comfortable being transported long distances. Even in comfortable vans, some of the alpacas show signs of stress. In extreme cases, they may stop eating altogether. It is therefore important that when buying, either buy an alpaca that is used to being transported around or just buy near your farm. In this way you won't have to worry about the negative effects of transporting alpacas for long distances.

Lastly, it's crucial that you ensure that the alpaca you buy has been well taken care of, so that bio-security risks are minimized. During shearing, breeding and shows, alpacas move from farm to farm. In that process, they may get infected with diseases and parasites. These parasites and diseases often get transferred to other alpacas as they move from farm to farm. In view of this risk, it is critical that you buy an alpaca from a farm that doesn't host many alpacas from different farms. Alpacas from such farms are likely to come with bio-security risks. In case the alpaca has a contagious disease, it is likely to infect other alpacas.

Treatment of alpacas is usually quite expensive. It is therefore advisable that the alpaca you buy be completely disease free. In order to ensure this is the case, ask for a full inventory of all the health records of the alpaca. The records should have information on all the diseases the alpaca has been treated against including worming treatments, its vaccinations and test results. It is only with this information that you can truly know whether the alpaca is healthy or not.

Chapter 3. Owning Alpacas as Pets

For those seeking an alpaca as a pet there are several things to consider. First, it is important to realize that alpacas are a herd animal and do best when pastured with other alpacas. With this in mind, it is best to have a minimum of two alpacas.

Pet quality male alpacas can be purchased for (£400) $500 each. Male alpacas should be gelded (castrated), but this is best done after the age of two. Failure to geld can lead to behavioral problems, mainly due to the effects of testosterone.

A couple of pet males can be kept quite inexpensively. Expenses will be a yearly vet exam, worming and vaccinations, shearing, and perhaps hay and feed supplements (depending on the location). A pet dog can easily be more expensive to keep than two male alpacas.

Kids love alpacas. It is a wonder to watch the delight on the face of a child when they first meet an alpaca. And, most alpacas have an affinity for children. For the small acreage landowner with children, alpacas may be a perfect match. Besides the opportunity to learn the basic skills and responsibilities needed to care for a pet, children can become involved in 4-H or FFA activities, and may even develop a life long interest in the fiber arts.

Owning Alpacas for Fiber Production

The fiber artist will probably look for an alpaca with a better yield of higher quality fleece that what the average pet quality alpaca will produce. Given this, the fiber artist will probably pay a slight premium for fiber quality alpacas.

There are many good quality male alpacas that fail to meet the high standard of being a herdsire. Many alpaca breeders will part with these animals for (£600) $750-(£ 1200) $1500 apiece. Such an alpaca might display some minor conformational defects, or in some cases more serious, but not life threatening, problems, while producing a very high quality fleece.

A good quality fiber alpaca might produce as much as 10 pounds of quality fleece a year. The fiber artist producing one-off hand made goods from this fleece might well recoup their investment in the alpaca within the first year.

Alpaca spins easily. It is free of lanolin, unlike sheep's wool. Many hand spinners produce yarn prior to washing the fleece, choosing instead to wash the finished yarn. It is not unusual for the uninitiated to confuse finished alpaca yarns with man-made fibers due to their high luster and smooth hand.

Managing a Small Scale Alpaca Operation

An increasing number of people have chosen to purchase alpacas as part of a change in lifestyle. Not interested in the competition of the show ring, or the hassles of a large scale marketing program, these individuals have found that a small herd of alpacas can produce supplemental income while providing the rewards, and tax benefits, of a small scale farm operation. Individuals choosing to enter the alpaca industry at this level will probably want to purchase two to four mid-quality female alpacas, and in time acquire a herdsire alpaca suitable to their goals.

These individuals are able to experience the joys of the birthing season. They find satisfaction in a close relationship with their alpacas. They are content to sell the occasional alpaca or two to like-minded souls.

In the present market, they can reasonably expect to sell male alpacas they produce as pet or fiber quality animals for enough to cover their annual operating expenses, while obtaining (£ 8) $10-(£ 1200) $15,000 for female alpacas that they choose to sell. They often choose to broker their females through larger or more competitive farms.

These alpaca breeders may be involved in the fiber arts, using all of the fiber produced on their farm. Alternately, they may develop other outlets for the alpaca fleece, selling to local fiber artists or contributing their annual clip to the national alpaca fiber cooperative.

These people have found that the magical alpaca provides many rewards that are not accessible to those caught in the rat race of urban living. They are able to take advantage of the tax benefits available to agricultural producers in the United States, including significant write-offs for their land and infrastructure, while producing a supplemental income for their household.

Becoming an Alpaca Industry Leader

To breed the best alpacas requires the best foundation herd stock available. This approach to entry into the alpaca industry requires a significant cash investment. Exceptional alpaca herdsires have sold for as much as (£200000) $250,000 at auction. Fine quality breeding females may be valued at (£16000) $20,000 - (£32000) $40,000. Many of the more renowned alpacas will never find their way to an auction block or a sales list.

Alpaca breeders at this level must invest a great deal of time and money into their operations. Besides the annual show circuit, marketing expenses are a significant expense. For these folks, alpacas are indeed a lifestyle, but not necessarily one that is tied to their land and their animals.

The popular belief is that alpaca breeders at this level are making major strides to improve the breed. Only time will tell if this is in fact true. Certainly these alpaca breeders have succeeded in creating animals that are pleasing to the eye of the public and the judges. These alpaca breeders are analogous to Thoroughbred horse breeders. Pedigree, form and rarity can add significant value to the animals these operations produce.

Remember our discussion on the Breeders vs. Fiber Market? While it is generally believed that there are many years left before the transition completely from a Breeder's Market to a Fiber Market, the industry has always anticipated this change. In order to guarantee longevity in the current market, secure success as a future fiber farm, and increase chances to continue to benefit from an elite breeding market, the serious alpaca breeder will focus on quality first and foremost, quantity second. If this is the course that you are exploring, you will be well advised to purchase the highest quality breeding stock that you can afford. In building a herd, quality genetics are so very much more important than numbers.

There will always be a market for animals at this level of the industry, but with maturity the competition will only increase. The risk and investment may be higher, but for many, this is the place to aim for in the alpaca industry.

Farms that embrace this route should carefully consider what they should you be doing during the Breeders' Market period to insure that they not only survive, but prosper as the industry transitions to a Fiber Market?

Focusing on Genetic Improvement through a Herdsire Operation

In virtually every mainstream livestock industry there are owners of prize animals that provide genetics across the breed. The alpaca industry will follow the same path. Commercial alpaca farms will seek out proven genetics to improve their herd's production qualities, or to create hybrid vigor, much as beef ranches or dairy farms do.

The alpaca breeder wishing to establish a stud farm will need to be knowledgeable in livestock breeding techniques and production qualities. They will need to demonstrate prescience about the direction the alpaca industry is headed in order to be able to breed and fix desirable qualities in their sires. The reputation of a stud farm will be based on the production qualities of the offspring produced. In the show ring, this will mean consistent wins in the Get of Sire and Produce of Dam classes.

The stud farm will be able to produce income from breeding fees as well as the sale of animals. The stud farmer will need to cull their herd to insure continual improvement, and it is likely that they will employ some level of line or in-breeding to set traits. These breeding practices entail their own set of unique risks. An alpaca stud farm will be a high risk venture, but with the potential for high returns.

Putting it all Together

You have just finished reading descriptions of reasons why people own alpacas. You now understand that the reasons are diverse and range from one extreme to another. Next, it's time for you to formulate your own reasons for wanting to own alpacas. Of course, your specific plan may include a combination of the above or may include others. The important thing is that you have identified your end goals so that you will set up your whole business operation with the end goals in mind. You will also want to consider if you want to replace a full-time income, or just supplement it. The nature of your specific goals will define the number and type of alpacas that you need, and the extent of your involvement. Speaking of alpaca type, what are the two types of alpaca's people talk about?

Huacayas or Suris: How Do I Choose?

At this point in your alpaca research you may or may not know that there are there are two types of alpacas.

Huacaya :

and Suri.

Some alpaca farms are successful in keeping both types while some concentrate on one or the other. What you decide may be dependent upon the type of alpaca operation you decide on. For many, it is just a personal preference. Some people fall in love with the fluffy teddy bear-appearance of the huacaya. After all, who can resist that adorable face!

We were attracted by the elegant style of the suri and the fact that they are much rarer in numbers in the U.S. Will the rarity of the suri allow it to hold its value longer years from now when the market transitions from a breeders' market to a fiber market? Who knows for sure, but it's a speculation we are betting on.

Each choice has its merits and something you read in this report may sway your decision one way or another. This is just another factor to consider in your overall business objectives.

Define Your Strategy

The business objectives you have identified will be achieved by one or more different routes based on the value of alpaca livestock and associated products.

The main income streams will be from:

a) Sale of livestock

b) Stud fees from herdsire breedings

c) Agistment (boarding of alpacas for others)

d) Brokering (selling someone else's alpacas)

e) Sale of fiber

f) Retail sale of alpaca clothing and products (farm shop and local fairs and events).

g) Not everyone will take part in all the activities, and some will find additional ways of generating income, but this is a realistic list with which to start.

Before defining your final plan on paper, you should research all aspects of alpaca ownership (see bibliography), and visit a number of farms. Learn what other people are doing, and how they are achieving their goals, and compare them with your own objectives. You should also consider what structure the business will need – if any. Is a sole proprietorship best for your situation or would a limited liability company (LLC) be more suitable? You need to talk to a financial adviser who has experience with agricultural accounts and the rural lifestyle to help you determine the answers to these questions. Do not rely on any existing adviser who lacks this experience. If you can find someone with experience with alpacas to consult with you will be even better prepared. Raising alpacas is not an inexpensive undertaking. Decide how much you can afford to dedicate to building a business that may take 4 or 5 years to start making a reasonable return on investment.

Author Lewis Carroll once said, "If you don't know where you are going, any road will take you there." Alpacas can be found at every price point and for every purpose. If one begins their journey with alpacas without clarity of purpose it can lead to serious, and expensive, realignments in the future.

Alpacas

You may already have a good understanding of the history and nature of alpacas; but, so that everyone starts from a common ground, this section provides a quick overview.

What are they?

The alpaca is a member of the Camelid family, related to llamas. It is a ruminant, with a gentle grazing habit. It is smaller than a llama, usually about 36 inches at the withers, and weighing between 150 and 200 lbs. The fiber is more lustrous and stronger than sheep's wool. It not only is up to 5 times warmer, it is softer than cashmere or angora, Alpaca has non-allergenic qualities, making it very useful for people who have problems wearing woolen garments.

The fiber has a range of over 22 colors, including black, white, maroon, brown, fawn, chocolate, and gray. It has a greater variety of colors and hues than any other natural fiber making it the most versatile dye-free material available. Alpaca garments are prized the world over, for their warmth, durability, and beauty.

Alpacas are without a doubt one of the most beautiful animals in the world. They have immediate appeal to everyone who sees them, and their inquisitive nature along with their gentle temperament makes them ideal livestock animals.

There are two different kinds of alpacas; the huacaya (pronounced wa-kí-a) with its characteristic fluffy and wooly appearance, and the suri with its long, silky and draping locks. As of the end of 2004, there were 62,000 alpacas registered in North America. Of that number, 51,000 were huacaya and 11,000 were suri_edn2. As you can see, the vast majority of alpacas are huacaya; about 90%, both worldwide and in the USA.

For over 6,000 years alpacas have been raised in South America, primarily in Peru. They have provided a source of luxurious fiber to the Peruvian Indians since the pre-Inca days, continuing through to the present day. Unfortunately, in the 1500s, the Spanish conquistadors almost eliminated these beautiful animals to make way for the sheep they brought with them. Many of the Indians fled to the higher reaches of the Andes, taking their alpacas with them. Over the hundreds of years since then, the animals have adapted to living in the harsh conditions found there becoming, in the process, one of the most efficient grazing animals in the world.

Since the mid-1980s, alpacas have been bred in the United States. Foundation herds were first established through a series of importations from Peru, Bolivia, and Chile. The original US alpaca farmers started breeding to establish an "American" alpaca. The Peruvian herds are primarily white or light fawn, as this is the fiber in most demand by the processing mills. To achieve the predominance of whites, the colored alpacas were culled from the breeding stock. As alpacas are eaten in South America (but not elsewhere), those that were not needed for breeding often met this fate. Other coloreds were exported to Chile, Argentina, and Bolivia.

In contrast, the colored animals are very much in demand in the US, despite the fact that their fleece is often less valuable for processing, particularly if it is from pinto or appaloosa animals. To-date, the American market has been dominated by "pretty" or unique appearing, animals, regardless of the quality of their fiber. This is starting to change, as people become more educated on the topic, and realize that the long term future of the industry depends on the quality of fiber produced in the national clip (annual shearing).

Today there are some 5000 alpaca farms in the USA. The industry association AOBA (Alpaca Owners and Breeders Association) has passed the 4100 member mark (December 2004). This is just a fraction of the potential, and while nobody knows for sure, it will probably take another 10 years before there is any leveling off of demand.

Herd Objectives

Once you have set down your business objectives, it is time to decide how to build your alpaca herd to meet them. For most people, the immediate appeal is the fact that the alpaca produces a cria each year, with the potential of recouping the initial investment if it is female. This fact, together with the compounding effect of keeping the females to breed in the herd, means that a modest herd of, say 5 animals (allow (£72000) $90,000), can grow to over 100 (worth (£1.4m) $1.8 million) in less than 10 years.

In what most people would see as a more reasonable horizon, perhaps 5 years, a starter herd of 5 bred females could grow to over 30 animals, worth around (£) $500,000.

The price you pay for your alpacas will vary tremendously, depending on whether you want show quality animals, fiber animals, or just breeding livestock. If you are building a fiber herd, you would want to concentrate on gelded males (wethers). These animals are the least expensive, maybe (£400) $500 to (£1600) $2000. At the other extreme, a valuable herdsire can sell for over (£280000) $350,000! The range for females is narrower, probably (£8000) $10,000 to (£36000) $45,000, depending on conformation, background, and production history.

In addition to defining the type and number of animals that you want, you will probably want to set some criteria for the fiber characteristics of your herd. Outstanding fiber production is the future of the alpaca industry so improvement in both quality and quantity should be an objective of every alpaca breeder.

When you are talking to farmers about their herd, ask for the fiber details. They should be able to provide this information on the alpaca for sale, if the animal is over a year old. Some of the important fiber characteristics you should look at are described below.

Before you decide that you want to keep alpacas, whether you are looking for a charming pet, a business endeavor or just a little bit of variety on your farm, you will find that it is in your best interests to learn everything that you can about them. These animals are graceful, sweet and, once you get to understand them a little bit, simple enough to care for. Make sure that you are thoroughly grounded in the basics before you decide to buy your first bred females.

Physical Characteristics

When people think of camelids, they think of the camels of Asia and Africa, the Dromedary and the Bactrian. However, this family includes several members from South and Central America as well, of which the alpaca is only one. The alpaca is a relatively compact animal, and though it resembles the llama, it is significantly smaller. An adult alpaca weighs between 100 and 170 pounds, with the males being heavier and taller than the females. They stand about 3 feet tall at the shoulder, and from a distance, they are easily identified by their abundant fleece and their rounded rump. The tail of an alpaca is set fairly low, giving its back a smooth curve.

Alpacas have no front teeth. Instead, their extremely mobile and split upper lips reach out to grasp the grass that they eat, yanking it up and cutting it with their lower teeth. Like all camelids, alpacas are ruminants, meaning that they chew regurgitated food to gain all of the nutrients from it. Alpacas have three stomachs instead of four, and when they are stressed, they can be prone to ulcers.

These small camelids have two toes on each foot, and though each toe does have a tough nail growing out of it, the pad of the foot is surprisingly soft to the touch, though the skin itself is quite tough. These strong, sensitive feet are adapted to a life in the perilous mountains, and they are also one of the great advantages for people who choose to keep alpacas. Alpacas are very light-footed, meaning that they will not trample your pasture or do undue damage to it beyond their foraging.

Perhaps the most interesting physical characteristic of the alpaca is its hair, which is known as fleece or fiber. Like sheep, alpacas are primarily kept for their fleece, which grows thick and soft. The fleece must be shorn once a year, and the result is a highly valuable fiber that is prized for spinning and weaving. Alpaca fiber is known to be far softer than sheep wool, without the prickle of sheep wool, and completely hypoallergenic.

Most people who have allergies to sheep wool are allergic to the lanolin, which is absent on alpaca fiber. There are more than 20 natural colors of

22

alpaca fiber, ranging from a lustrous pure white to a deep black. In between, there are various shades of silver mixed with brown and some beautiful patterns as well. White alpaca fiber is the most common, as it is the fiber that is the simplest to dye.

Herd Behavior

Alpacas are naturally herd animals, and there are cases of alpacas who are kept on their own suffering from issues of poor health. They live in very close family groups, and in general, you will find most of your alpacas clustered together in the field.

Because they are prey animals, alpacas band together very tightly for protection. At any given time, the bulk of the herd is foraging and eating, while a few animals are playing lookout.

Before they were domesticated, the alpaca herd's survival largely depended on how close the members could stay together. This has led to an adaptation that is very handy for alpaca keepers. Alpacas tend to have a communal dung heap. They all defecate and urinate in the same place, and often, they do at the same time as well! This trait makes it very easy to keep their paddock tidy. Their dung is nearly odorless, and if it is used cautiously, it is ideal for composting.

A single warning cry, which is a high-pitched unmistakable shriek, will cause the alpaca herd to take flight or to bundle together, all looking for danger.

Left to their own devices, males and females alpacas will live in communal herds. There is one dominant male who rules over a harem of females. The dominant male will battle other males to remain dominant, and these fights can harm the animals and even result in death.

Overall, it is far better to keep alpacas in sex-segregated herds until it is time to breed them Left to their own devices and without the presence of females, the males, known as machos, will live a peaceful and companionable bachelor existence. The females, known as hembras, are known for being especially docile and sociable.

Another reason to keep males and females separated is because there is no such thing as an alpaca mating season. The females can come into heat any time they are close to males, and this can lead to unplanned pregnancies at a time when you are not prepared for them.

Alpacas have a fairly rich language of vocalizations that they use to communicate with one another. For example, there is a gentle hum that is used to signal a wide variety of low-intensity things. The hum might be a call to another herd animal, an expression of curiosity or an expression of anxiety. Males have a mating cry that is rather deeper and throaty, called orgling. There are also a wide variety of screams and screeches, which are used defensively or aggressively.

Males vs. Females

The question of whether to purchase male or female alpacas is one that is heavily dependent on your situation and what you want the alpacas for. While it is possible to keep a single alpaca, it is highly recommended that you keep at least two animals of the same sex.

In terms of personality, both hembras and machos tend to be stand-offish at first and then more friendly when they get to know you. Males tend to be more curious and friendly at first than females, but females can be similarly sweet after they have gotten to know you

Fiber Structure

In order to make informed decisions on selecting quality foundation herd animals with desirable fiber characteristics, the new alpaca breeder must understand basic fiber anatomy and physiology. This section provides information that will help you understand the differences between suri and huacaya fiber what makes a good fiber producing alpaca. Alpaca fiber is composed of three distinct elements; the cuticle or scale, the cortical cells and an intracellular binder to hold it all together. A complex protein called keratin forms the composition of the fiber. The fiber itself is a complex assembly made up of a vast number of cells.

The inside of the fiber consists entirely of rounded elongated and spindle shaped cells called cortical cells. Cortical cells are thick in the middle and taper away to a point at each end. The outer cells (cuticle) are hard flattened scale-like cells which do not fit evenly together. The edges, of these cells protrude from the fiber shaft giving the fiber a serrated edge.

Alpaca fleece is graded into various categories, based on the micron count. The criteria for these can vary somewhat between processors, but this following list is a good guideline:
1) Royal <20 microns
2) Baby 21 - 23 microns

3) Standard 24 - 28 microns
4) Adult 29 - 32 microns
5) Coarse 33 - 35 microns
6) Very Coarse > 35 microns

There is a trade-off between the fineness of the fiber and the weight of the blanket. In many cases, particularly at the very finest level, the premium paid for the fine micron count is not sufficient to make up for the loss of weight.

Standard Deviation

Standard deviation is a calculation designed to indicate how consistent the micron count is distributed throughout the sample being tested. Put simply, a standard deviation describes where 68% of the fibers lie in relation to the mean fiber diameter of the sample. The mean fiber diameter is the value where half the fibers have a smaller diameter and half the fibers have a larger diameter.

Standard Deviation (S.D.) is measured and quoted in microns. So, a standard deviation of 4.0 microns means that 68% of the fibers from the sample fall within the 4.0 micron range. Breeding goals should include decreasing the S.D. of the herd because the lower the S.D. the more consistent the fiber diameter.

Co-efficient of Variation

Co-efficient of variation (C.V.) is a calculation expressed as a % which is designed to give an alternative method of describing evenness of micron in a sample. It also allows comparisons between samples that are more accurate and reliable than standard deviation alone. For example, an S.D. of 3.5 on a 30 micron fiber sample is a much better reflection of consistency than an S.D. on a 15 micron sample where the S.D. represents a much larger proportion of the mean.

C.V. allows a breeder to look at like animals and compare them within a herd under the same management and environmental conditions. Exceptional finer fleeces with reflect low C.V. with values under 20% being highly desirable and reflective of superior fleece.

Comfort Factor

Generally speaking, fibers with a diameter greater than 30 microns create a prickle sensation when worn against the skin. The value of the comfort factor is determined by subtracting the percentage of fibers with a diameter greater than 30 microns from 100%. For example, if the percentage of fibers greater than 30 microns is 3%, then the comfort factor is 100% - 3% or 97%

Breeding Goals

Each breeder should have specific fiber characteristics that they are trying to achieve. These can be described in a herd breeding plan. An example is given below.

In their herd breeding plan, farm XYZ has created fiber criteria of as indicated in the table below. These are the standards they have set to measure the success of their breeding program. In order to achieve these standards, they will cull from the breeding program any animal that does not meet them.

Farm XYZ Fiber Criteria	Measurement
Shear weight	8 lbs or over at 2 years (5.5+ lbs of which is from the blanket area)
Length of staple	6+ inches
AFD Yearling	16.0 – 22.0 μ
AFD Adults	18- 25 μ
AFD Adult over 5 years old	<28 μ
Standard Deviation S.D.	<4.0
Co-efficient of Variation C.V.	<20.0
Comfort Factor	>97%

In this illustration, AFD refers to Average Fiber Diameter – the thickness of individual fibers. Anything under 25 microns (μ) is regarded as good. Whatever figures you decide upon, they should only be used as a guide. Many different factors can influence the figures, including age, diet, environmental conditions, health, and pregnancy.

Again, the farmers to whom you are talking should be able to explain this to you. Words of caution however, beware of anyone saying that these figures are unimportant, and that it is only "hand" (the way the fleece feels) that matters. While hand is important, particularly in the show ring, the measured figures are the only definitive, accurate basis for comparison. Just be sure to compare like with like.

Culling

When breeding for genetic improvement, your goal is for the cria produced to be an improvement of its dam. Animals that do not conform to your standards should be culled, by selling them to other breeders (their objectives may differ from yours), or as companion or fiber animals. Note: Culled does not mean killed, in this instance!
Obviously, any animals that exhibit undesirable characteristics should not be bred.

Farm Infrastructure

Even before your first alpaca arrives, you have plenty of work to do! Alpacas are easy on the environment, do not challenge fences, and require little in the way of permanent shelter. However, you still need to make some arrangements in all of these areas.

Fencing

You may have heard that alpacas do not challenge fences. While this may generally be true, we have heard of exceptions to this rule of thumb. There have been reports of breeding males leaping over a 4 foot fence in order to attack other males that they perceived as invading their territory. There have also been fence failures due to large males rubbing themselves against the fence, and various calamities such as trees being blown down on a fence and even the collapse of a shelter onto a fence in a wind storm. The bottom line – build a sturdy fence.

One of the primary purposes of fencing is to prevent predators from accessing your herd. The type and number of predators will vary according to your area. In most localities, wild dogs are a major threat, followed by coyotes; but do not disregard the neighbors' dogs. The most common attacks are from someone's pet!

There are many fencing options to choose from and every alpaca farmer you talk to has his or her own ideas on fencing. I am no different. I believe the perimeter fencing should be the most secure to protect against outside penetration. The exterior fencing should be a minimum of 5 feet high. It should be constructed of a sturdy, woven fence material to serve as barrier protection. Many alpaca owners have opted for no-climb horse fencing (2"x4" mesh) which is very effective but, but quite expensive and difficult to install. I have found that there are more economical choices that are just as safe and effective if installed correctly.

I believe that a 48 inch high woven wire field fence with 2 strands of HT (high tensile) wire across the top to make a total height of 5 ft. is sufficient. Considering reliability, maintenance, cost, appearance and reduction of risk, this is one the best multi-species boundary fence designs available. If going with this choice, the opening size of the weave is critical. Use woven wire with verticals every 9 inches. If the verticals are spaced every 12 inches, crias and small dogs can pass through.

Verticals every 6 in. can entrap an alpaca's head, resulting in serious injury or death. I also recommend installing one or two electrified offset strands on the grazing side of the fence for even more protection. Recently, there has been material published touting the benefits of offset hot wires.

Five Reasons to Offset all "Hot" wires in Permanent Fences:

1) You can use smaller energizers that are less costly and safer. Powerful energizers are only needed to overwhelm the high energy drain that occurs in spring and summer from high vegetative contact. Offsetting all energized wires reduces this drain by up to 90% and eliminates the need for the high joule unit.

2) To cut fence maintenance--no weed concerns means few voltage worries. Checking the voltage can be done monthly instead of daily.

3) To keep predators out (if one of the offset wires is low enough) and guard dogs in.

4) To keep alpacas from getting heads caught in the woven wire.

6) To reduce liability and risk from the public receiving a nasty "shock." To contact a hot wire offset on the inside of your boundary fence the public must trespass.

Why is offset wire effective?

▪ In a boundary fence (along a road, forest or crop field), the woven and non-energized woven and HT wire on the outside of the fence posts act as a physical barrier to prevent brush, vines and ungrazed tall, heavy, wet grass from touching or falling onto hot wires--even if they are close to the ground.

▪ Because only 1 or 2 offset wires are installed, alpacas are able to graze grass below the hot wires. It's important to understand that fences with too many hot wires prevent this natural animal "herbicide" activity from occurring.

How many wires should be energized?

One wire at 24 in. will keep most adult alpacas from contacting the fence. To keep coyotes out and guard dogs in use 2 wires (8 in. and 28 in.). Always disconnect the lower wire whenever coyote risk is low--this reduces the risk of humans contacting the lower wire and allows your alpacas to graze back the weeds and brush around it.

To deter dogs and coyotes from digging under the fence, raise the woven wire up 2 in. and install a HT barbed wire at ground level. Never use barbed wire higher than ground level on the grazing side of the fence. Alpaca's bulky fleece can easily become caught in the barbs resulting in serious injury or death. In areas with large predators (cougar or bear) additional steps may be necessary. Check with other local livestock owners to see what they recommend.

For cross-fencing to divide pastures, something less substantial can be used. The main purpose for this type of fencing is to keep the alpacas separate from each other. Some people choose to use the same design as the perimeter fence described above, only at a 4 ft. height. Whatever you choose to use, keep in mind the intended purpose and make sure you are comfortable with the characteristics of each type.

Proper fencing design facilitates efficient use of your pastures. Several small paddocks are better than just a couple of large pastures. Ideally, you will want at least 6 small paddocks for each group of alpacas that you plan to run. This will allow for effective pasture rotation and is important for parasite control. If you have a substantial amount of fencing to install, it is important to spend some time working out exactly where you will keep the various segregated groups of alpacas. For example, the males need to be kept away from the females, pregnant females should be separated from the rest of the herd, and mothers with crias form another group. You may also need areas for quarantining visiting alpacas, and for sick or convalescing animals. This doesn't need as much land as it may seem!

Talk to an experienced breeder to discuss the best plan for your situation. The layout should be designed to facilitate the movement of animals from one area to another, as well as ensuring that they all have access to food, water and shelter, at all times. Time spent planning these elements will be amply repaid when you have a well-designed facility to make your daily tasks easier. Effective fencing for an alpaca farming operation is art and science. It is not significantly different than any other livestock operation. Therefore, the wise alpaca farmer will seek advice from other, experienced livestock farmers.

Gates

It seems that there are never enough gates. There is nothing more frustrating than standing ten feet from a piece of trash that needs to be picked up from the pasture, but having to walk two hundred yards to get to it - down the fence to the nearest gate and then back up to where the trash is.

There are several options when choosing gates. The most common are made from tubular steel with horizontal bars. The problem with these is that small dogs and coyotes can squeeze through the bars and invade your herd. If you use this type of gate, be sure to attach a woven or welded wire section of fence to the gate for added protection. We use gates that already have the welded 2x4 wire panel attached. These work great, provide the extra protection against predators and are light weight. Be sure that your gates are wide enough to allow access by your equipment. All gates should be a minimum of 10 feet.

Gates are the most expensive part of a fence. If sufficient gates do not fit in the budget, plan your fences for their future addition. It is far easier to set posts before the wire is strung. This will allow you to simply cut out a section of fencing, tie it off to the existing posts, and hang your gate.

Guard Animals

In areas where there is a serious predator threat, the use of livestock guard dogs (LGD) or guard llamas can be considered.

Shelter

With their origins in the harsh lands of the Altiplano in Peru, alpacas are hardy creatures, well able to withstand the cold of North American winters. They have more trouble in the hot and humid summers. The danger point for them arises with a combination of the temperature and humidity. A common way of assessing the risk is to combine the two figures and, if the result nears 160 (e.g. temperature 90F and humidity 70%), then the alpacas are in danger. At this point they will need external cooling with fans and/or belly sprinklers or wading pools.

In view of the need to keep cool in the summer, and their hardiness in the winter, a three sided structure, with plenty of open spaces for airflow, is the optimum building for the alpacas' shelter. The open side should be away from the prevailing wind. Consider incorporating the following features into your design:

1) A floor space of 10' x 20' can over winter approximately eight alpacas. This assumes they will have free access to pasture most of the time.

2) Skids underneath a stand-alone shed add great flexibility. If the ground inside becomes too messy (after a long winter), you can move the shed to a new site. Skids make it easy to move to a new pasture or just change positions with the seasons.

3) Tarping the front opening smaller in winter will help with tricky winds and drifting snow. Using clear tarps will let the sun inside. Sun in the winter is always a healthy plus. A bed of straw will maximize protection from severe cold.

4) A gate for the entrance will turn your shelter into a catch pen. Locating your feed trays in the shed will help greatly in catching your alpacas.

5) Higher ceiling will also have an advantage of creating space for a small hay storage shelf.

6) It can be a plus to have an enclosed pen just outside your shed. This space would have a crushed gravel surface. In spring or fall when the pasture is wet and muddy, your alpacas can exercise and take up the healthy sunshine and still stay clean.

Many people find that a combination of a large barn for the main structure, and smaller shelters in the pastures, is ideal. The large barn should have a work room for veterinary examinations and routine procedures that could also double as an office. There should be space for feed, hay and tack storage as well. In colder climates, you may want to consider an enclosed, insulated and heated area that could be used as a sick room. Consider the following features for this versatile room:

7) Size this room as large as possible. A 10' x 20' space would be good for 3 adults with crias. Smaller rooms can work successfully but the more space your alpacas have the more trouble-free your operation will be.

8) Insulate as well as possible. Be sure to keep friable materials out of reach. Young alpacas may nibble on insulation, etc. Heavy insulation is

great but do not seal this space tight. Good ventilation is critical. A newborn cria can die from ammonia fumes from alpaca urine.

9) Heat with a thermostatically controlled heater and maintain approximately 40°F. If your heater produces combustion gases they must be vented outside. Adequate make-up air must be provided for burner type heaters. Do not use radiant light bulb type heat, as this U.V. light can burn the eyes and skin. An ideal set-up would provide radiant heat through the floor via circulating hot water pipes.

10) We use overhead electric radiant fixture. These are hung from the ceiling to keep them well out of the reach of the alpacas. All combustibles are kept away. A thermometer on the wall is a must.
Depending on the proximity of the barn to other facilities, you may also want to consider installing telephone, fax, and computer equipment. It is also very useful to have a closed circuit television capability.

Video Monitoring

A closed circuit video system is a simple video setup used to monitor your alpacas from almost anywhere. Using this technology is particularly valuable when you are on "cria watch". While alpacas generally give birth mid-morning to early afternoon, some are born when you least expect it. Having the ability to monitor birthing progress from the house saves countless trips to the barn to check out what going on with that new mom-to-be. Then, once the cria is born, you will be able to comfortably check in on them from a distance to allow mom and cria to bond without human intervention.

The latest in wireless barn camera technology makes installation simple and convenient. These systems can be placed up to 1 mile away from your TV or computer with an extra high power transmitter and 2.4 Ghz systems penetrate right through walls and floors. Special systems are available for metal barns and trailers.

Once you have your camera up and running, you can post still or full motions images on the internet so that you can watch from work, or when you're away from home. All you need is a computer with an internet connection (broadband is best but not required), a video capture card, Webcam Software, and a web Page.

Land

The choice of land for an alpaca operation can be based more on the convenience and choice of the owner than on the need of the animals. However, if one intends to diversify their farm operation, they should select farm land that is suitable for their overall plans.

Many sources will state that one can keep as many as 10 alpacas per acre. With irrigation and good forage this is true, but a more reasonable figure is probably 5-7 alpacas per acre.

The best land for an alpaca farming operation will be similar to that for any other livestock farm. Flat land with deep rich soils will provide a number of advantages, including the ease and flexibility of fencing and the use of farm equipment. Water availability should always be a factor when selecting suitable land. Some States will not allow the use of domestic water supplies for irrigating farm land or watering livestock. Check your local regulations before committing yourself to a piece of land or a herd of alpacas!

Forage for your alpacas is another consideration. Alpacas are "browsers" and will sample almost anything that is growing. It is important to be sure that your land is free of toxic plants. Problem plants can be identified with the help of your local Extension office. Information can also be found on the Internet.

How much land is needed will be dependent upon the goals of the individual alpaca farm. A five acre parcel can provide four acres of pasture, which will sustain 20-30 alpacas with proper pasture management. Keep in mind though; if these are breeding females the load on the pasture will be greater due to the production of cria. Also consider that multiple paddock construction and rotational practices will limit the amount of pasture that is available on any one time. (This sounds pretty basic, but there have been a number of examples of folks running out of land due to poor planning on this simple point.)

It is also important to plan for herd management, which requires keeping males separate from females, providing an area for weaning, and preferably providing a quarantine area for alpacas that have left your property.

33

Pastures

The diet of alpacas in their homeland tends to be sparse grasses with low nutritional value. That has led to them being one of the most efficient animals for grazing. They convert 80% of what they eat into energy. Unfortunately, in the US they are often too well-fed, leading to them becoming "over-conditioned" or in other words, fat!
As with people, obesity endangers their health, as well as making it more difficult to conceive, and to hold a pregnancy. It can also lead to dystocia (birthing problems). It is also believed that fiber coarsens as the animal carries more fat. This has been validated by a number of studies that also demonstrated that the fiber will improve as the animal returns to a healthier weight.

Forage makes up 80% plus of the healthy alpacas' diet. Pasture and hay quality for alpaca owners seems to fit two extremes. It is either poor quality or extremely high quality. Obviously, it is best not to get to the point where special dietary needs have to be considered, so forage testing is a necessity for alpaca health. The way to achieve this is to analyze the nutritional requirements for the herd, and then review the properties of the soil and grass to identify the need for supplements. Your local agricultural agent can help with these analyses. The results of the soil sampling may well indicate that you need to add fertilizer and lime to the land. This can be done in the fall or spring, if needed, and can be combined with over-seeding with new grass.

An adult alpaca will usually need about 1½% of its body weight in food intake each day. This will normally be provided by grazing, supplemented with good quality hay. A handful of alpaca pellets, and free access to mineral supplement granules complete their dietary needs. Of course, the herd must have access to fresh water at all times.

When preparing alpaca pastures and fencing, the size of the pasture, the use of the animal and the stocking density need to be considered. Will the pasture be for males or producing females? Good pasture can support 8 to 10 males and 6 to 8 females per acre. The pasture should be well drained, properly fenced, contain adequate shade, and have a plentiful supply of fresh water, free of excessive iron and sulfur.

Pasture rotation is a part of any good management program. Rotation creates pasture rest and growth efficiency as well as aiding in parasite control. Adequate paddocks should be available to allow pasture rotation and field rest every three weeks. If the pasture is very lush and abundant, controlled grazing may be necessary, especially if the grazing alpaca's body score is between 5 and 6. They may need to forage only 3-4 hours per day.

The best grass for the pastures is usually orchard grass. Most professionally-formulated alpaca supplements balance well with orchard grass. It works nicely in combination other grasses or up to 20% alfalfa. Orchard grass usually lasts 4 to 5 years. Orchard grass alone or in the same combination makes great hay, which preferably should be second cut. Fescue grass is to be avoided, as it can carry an endophytic fungus that can cause abortions or death.

Clean-up

Alpacas tend to mark one or two areas in the pasture for communal dung piles, and they will then all use the same places. This makes it very easy to clean up after them. Their efficient digestive system extracts virtually everything but the fiber from the food they consume, so the manure consists of virtually odorless, dry pellets, much like rabbit or sheep droppings. Alpaca manure is fantastic fertilizer, either raw for trees and shrubs or as compost for vegetable crops. It is so low in nitrogen that it will not burn plants even if used on the garden immediately. There may even be a small market for selling composted alpaca manure in your area. As a local supplier of wholesome farm nutrients, your product could become a great asset to small-scale sustainable agriculture in your area.

Healthy soils are living soils, and alpaca manure can be a key ingredient in depleted soils, transforming them into a rich medium capable of growing nutritious food.

Chapter 4. Alpaca Husbandry

The first rule of alpaca husbandry is that these herd animals are best kept in pairs. Beyond that, however, these are marvelously adaptable animals, adjusting to a wide range of climates with the correct help from their keepers.

Visit Alpaca Farms

If you are completely new to the alpaca industry and have never lived on or owned a farm or a ranch, there's no denying the fact that you have a lot to learn! Reading this book is a good start, but there is absolutely no substitute for making friends with people in the industry who live and work with alpacas daily.

Either by attending alpaca shows, or reaching out to existing alpaca farmers in your area, it will be greatly to your benefit to cultivate a mentor or mentors. This will allow you to get hands on experience, discuss pros and cons of equipment, shelters, veterinary care, feed — all the daily details of being an alpaca owner! And you'll have someone to call when something comes up you didn't anticipate or don't know how to handle! Never underestimate the importance of being able to make that phone call. I think you'll find that alpaca people tend to be a pretty clannish and close-knit bunch. You should have no trouble making new friends, and learning the industry from the inside.

Take the following husbandry information as a primer in the basics so you can go in armed with specific questions. I can't stress strongly enough the need to conduct research and prepare your facilities fully BEFORE you purchase your first alpacas.

Purchasing Alpacas

Although there are many criteria that can be applied to the purchase of an alpaca, you will want to consider some of the following general points:

Choose animals that have a pleasing appearance to the eye, including straight legs and a body shape that is well balanced.

Over the "blanket" area, which is essentially the area that would be covered by a saddle blanket on a horse and down the sides toward the belly, the fleece should have an even texture.

You should only be able to see guard hairs on the front "bib" or chest and potentially some on the neck.

If purchasing a male for breeding purposes, make certain the testicles are equal in size.

Buy only from reputable breeders with a solid record in the show ring and see references from satisfied clients.

Upon purchase, you should receive some form of "handover" report that includes information like date of birth, injections received, mating dates if applicable, and ultrasound dates if applicable.

All breeding stock should come with veterinary health certificates which will be necessary for insurance purposes. Pregnant females are generally sold with some form of a live birth guarantee and stud males with a fertility guarantee.

Providing Shelter

In the vast majority of cases, providing a three-sided shelter with one open side, usual on the east to southeast side works well for alpacas as it does for many kinds of livestock.

The reasoning on the positioning of the open side is to shelter the animals from cold north winds and rain while giving them easy and unencumbered access. This arrangement can, of course, vary by region.

The construction of the shelter can follow any number of designs appropriate to region and circumstances. If the shelter is to be temporary, stacked straw bales covered by a tarp is an inexpensive approach. In more permanent circumstances, barns are used, often with heated floors and automatic watering and misting systems, especially in breeding operations.

Space is the most important consideration. Allow 20-30 square feet / 1.86-2.8 m2 per alpaca.

Concrete floors, if possible, have a distinct advantage, especially when drains are incorporated into the design for washing out urine. Dirt and crushed stone or gravel has to be periodically removed. Typically straw bedding is provided, especially in the cold months, which also must be "mucked" out to keep it clean of accumulated urine.

Neither wood shavings nor sawdust is a good choice for flooring or bedding material for use with alpacas. Both cause debris in the fiber that lowers the quality of the fleece at shearing time.

Methods of Cooling

Alpacas need shade in the summer to escape the heat of the day, but even on the hottest days you'll find these animals lying on their sides taking in the full sun. This can be disconcerting for first-time alpaca owners, but like cats, alpacas love a good sun bath and will stay there until their fleece is almost too hot to touch.

If you opt for a fan in the barn / shelter, be careful to buy one that is specifically designed for agricultural use. The housing must be capable of keeping high levels of dust out of the motor compartment or the unit will be highly susceptible to overheating, which is a significant fire hazard.

Don't shop for a fan in your local department or discount store. Go to a farm store or agricultural catalog. The cost will be greater, but the safety factor is an imperative. In more arid regions, the use of misters for cooling is quite common, and also highly effective. Other cooling techniques include sprinklers, soaker hoses, and damp patches of sand.

Alpacas should not have access to ponds or deep water, however, as soaking will cause the fleece to rot and break. If the fiber becomes matted from being wet, heat cannot dissipate from the skin and the potential for overheating will increase. Bodies of water can also be a vector for the transmission of disease and parasites.

In the winter, any body of standing water in a pasture is a significant hazard to the alpacas. They can easily slip on the ice, fall through, and drown.

Fencing and Other Protective Measures

The number of fenced areas or pastures you will require for you alpacas depends on whether or not you will be breeding the animals. If so, you will need to plan for 3-4 fenced areas:

1) one to house the females
2) one to house the males

3) one for young males to protect them from aggression
4) one for animals just weaned

Under the best possible circumstances you will have enough land to rotate the animals through a series of pastures to prevent too much grazing and to allow the available forage to recuperate.

If you show alpacas, you may also want to have a quarantine pasture for the animals routinely moved on and off the land to guard against the spread of any infectious diseases.

The purpose of fencing with alpacas is primarily for containment and to keep predators out rather than to keep your alpacas in. They are very passive animals and unlike other types of livestock, will not challenge fences.

Material Considerations

In choosing your fencing materials, remember that alpacas have long necks and exhibit a tendency to stick their heads through open spaces. Traditional cattle fencing with net wire on the bottom and 2-3 single strands on the top offers too many enticing gaps for alpaca.

No-climb horse fencing (welded mesh) works well, as do cyclone (chain link) fences. Try to avoid "New Zealand" or high tensile fences made of single strands of wire at spaced horizontal intervals. Never use barbed wire, and use plastic fencing as a temporary expediency only.

If you can afford to do so, consider having a perimeter fence for predator control that is at least 5 feet / 1.5 meters high. Six feet / 1.8 meters is even better.

For predators with a tendency to dig under fences, bury mesh wire to a depth of at least one foot / 0.3 meters. Electrified fencing is also an option on the perimeter.

Use alpaca safe materials for the interior fence at a height of 4-5 feet / 1.2-1.5 meters.

(Note that the use of guard dogs with your alpacas can be an excellent security boost in areas with high predator activity.)

Diet and Nutrition

Alpacas need amazingly little to survive. On their native ranges in Chile, Peru, and Bolivia, they only have access to lush grasses during the rainy season. The rest of the year, they subsist on sparse vegetation only.

In pastures with an adequate cover of natural, non-fertilized grasses, alpacas will graze contentedly and usually thrive. A mix of 4-6 grasses in a pasture is ideal to create a varied foraging environment. Typically used grasses include:

- Brome
- Orchard
- Timothy
- Endophyte-free Fescue
- Winter Wheat
- Bluegrass
- Bermuda
- Millet
- Sudan Grass
- Bahia Grass

Typically a two-week rotation schedule (depending on region) is enough to allow grass to replenish itself. Supplement natural grasses with a low-protein grass hay.

On a daily basis, alpacas eat 1.5% to 2% of their body weight by volume, so a 150 lb. / 68 kg alpaca would need to consume roughly 3 lbs. / 1.4 kg. About 60% of that intake should be from grazing.
The remaining 40% of the diet should come from commercially prepared alpaca feed. This ensures that the animals get vitamins and minerals, like selenium, that can't always be obtained from grass and hay alone.

Although there are many options, an exemplar feed is Mazuri Alpaca & Llama Maintenance Diet, which, according to the packaging, is "designed to maintain adult alpacas & llamas in good condition. This product is not designed for growing, gestating or lactating animals or for fiber animals. It's designed to complement grass or legume hay/pasture."

The suggested feeding directions on the product are, "To be fed with free-choice alfalfa or grass hay or pasture. In order to meet NRC recommendations for new world camelids, animals being fed hay should consume this product at a rate of 0.5 lb. pellet {0.22 kg} per 100 lbs. {45 kg} of body weight (BW).

Hydration

Provide your alpacas with a source of clean, fresh water near their shelter at all times. Although these animals do not consume large amounts of water, they will refuse to drink altogether if their water is dirty or stale.

Shearing

Thanks to the Internet, it's quite easy to go to YouTube and watch any number of videos of alpacas being sheared. The process begins with isolating the alpaca in a contained space called a "catch pen" and then taking the animal into a shearing barn with a concrete floor.

This keeps the fleece as free of debris as possible and allows for better clean-up. The animals are laid flat on their side and the fleece is shorn with electric clippers.

Power Shears

These power shears are made up of a hand piece, comb, and cutters. Portable shears with the motor contained in the handle are recommended for alpacas.

Good quality commercial models that can handle the dense alpaca fleece cost (£200) $250-(£400) $500.

The adjustable comb attaches to the hand piece. The flat side faces up and away from the animal. Its purpose is to enter and separate the fibers. This piece dulls quickly, and must be replaced after 2 or 3 animals are shorn. Combs cost (£12) $15-(£28) $35each.

The cutters typically have four triangular points. They attach to the hand piece and press firmly against the comb. Cutters dull even faster than combs, at the rate of about three cutters per single comb. Cutters cost (£8) $10-(£12) $15.

Shearing Techniques

Although there are many techniques for shearing animals, some unique to the individual, the basic procedure is that the animal is laid on its side and the shearer works from the belly toward the center of the back.

The fleece is taken off as one single piece or "blanket." The preference is to remove the fleece in one unit, cutting as close to the skin as possible. After one side is completed, the animal is flipped to the other side and the procedure is repeated. It usually takes three people working as a team, one holding the head and shielding the eyes, and two removing the fleece.

(Many alpaca owners far prefer to hire professional shearers to complete this task.)

The hair is left long on the head and legs, so a shorn alpaca looks a bit like it's wearing a wig and old-fashioned ladies' pantaloons!

(While it is certainly possible for a single person to shear an animal, which requires a fair degree of both experience and confidence. Anyone with experience shearing sheep will have no difficulty shearing an alpaca.)

Shearing and Heat Stress

Even if you are keeping alpacas as pets, the animals should be shorn each year. Failure to do so increases the risk of fatal heat stress. At best, a male that has suffered heat stress can be left permanent by sterile. Signs of heat stress include:

- a wobbling gait
- flaring of the nostrils
- open mouth breathing
- a refusal to stand from the kush position

The best method to alleviate heat stress is to remove the fleece from the body and then the neck. Pour isopropyl alcohol over the body and put the alpaca in front of a fan. If no alcohol is available, cool water will help. Do not hose down a fully fleeced alpaca as the fiber will mat and prevent heat release.

A vet should be consulted as the animal may need treatment, including injections of Banamine and B-complex vitamins.

Alpaca Judging

Like all exhibition shows for pedigreed animals or exceptional livestock, alpaca shows are organized by various governing bodies in the industry. These will vary by region, but there are opportunities for enthusiasts of all ages from children to adults to compete with their animals.

In general, alpaca judges look for the following points:

1) Quality of movement when walking toward and away.
2) Absence of physical anomalies or abnormalities.
3) Width of the chest.
4) Nature of boning (fine or heavy.)
5) Quality of the top line (Strong or frail and humped back.)
6) Fullness of the cap.
7) Shape of the ears.
8) Shape of the head (wedge.)
9) Fullness of a Huacaya's cheeks.
10) Quality of the fleece.

After observing the animals and forming an initial impression, judges conduct a hands-on evaluation before placing the class. Although there are set points to take into consideration, alpaca judging is as much an art as a science and there is almost always disagreement with the judges' final decision!

The Matter of Breed Standards

Although there is no one set breed standard for alpacas, the following points are used by the International Alpaca Judging School. They are reproduced here as an example of the criteria used in evaluating the quality of alpaca show animals. Depending on your location in the world, other standards may apply. (*Source:* "A Comparative Analysis of Alpaca Breed Type and Standards," by Jude Anderson, Maggie Krieger, and Mike Safley, which can be accessed at the Alpaca Library at www.alpacas.com/AlpacaLibrary.)

General Appearance – Huacayas

The ideal Huacaya alpaca has a squared-off appearance with four strong legs. It is a graceful, well-proportioned animal with the neck being two-thirds of the length of the back and the legs matching the length of the neck. It is well covered with fiber from the top of the head to the toes. It has fiber characteristics that differ distinctly to the Suri alpaca.

General Appearance – Suris

The ideal Suri alpaca has a squared off elegant appearance with four strong legs. It is a graceful, well-proportioned animal with the neck being two-thirds of the length of the back and the legs matching the length of the neck. It is well covered with fiber from the top of the head to the toes. It has fiber characteristics that differ distinctly to the Huacaya alpaca.

Head – Huacayas

The head is neatly formed of medium length with a square muzzle. It bears two upright spear-shaped ears between which there is a full fiber topknot or bonnet. The eyes protrude slightly from their sockets and are large and round. The eyes can be of several shades although 90% of the population have black eyes. The other acceptable color is brown. There are also various shades of blue eyes with or without colored flecks. The jaws fit together well, with the lower incisors meeting the upper dental pad. The upper lip is centrally divided and mobile to give them more dexterity in gathering food from certain plants.

The nose has two well-defined flaring nostrils. Darker pigmentation to the skin is preferred around the mouth and eyes giving them added protection to ultra-violet light radiation and the environment.

Major Faults:

1) Deafness in blue-eyed alpacas with lack of skin pigmentation and white fleece.
2) Gopher ears.
3) Superior and inferior prognathism.
4) Wry face.
5) Lump on the side of the face indicative of abscessing in the mouth.
6) Eyes: cataracts, entropy, ectropy, blindness.

Minor Faults:

1) A straight inside border or banana-type configuration of the ear (indicating llama traits).
2) Forward set ears.
3) Roman nose (llama tendency).
4) Narrow head.
5) Muffled face in the adult alpaca. (fiber or hair impeding the alpaca's vision).
6) Open-faced. (Lack of fiber coverage over the face.)
7) Lack of pigmentation on the lips and around the eyes.
8) Retained or persistent deciduous teeth.

Head - Suris

The head is neatly formed of medium length with a square muzzle. Suris have more of a tapering shape to the muzzle. They bear two upright spear-shaped ears between which there is a full fiber topknot or bonnet that falls typically in a fringe over the brow. Suri ears are approximately 2cm longer than Huacaya ears.

The eyes protrude slightly from their sockets and are large and round. The eyes can be of several shades although 90% of the population is black. Brown is also a desirable color. There are also various shades of blue with or without colored flecks.

The jaws fit together well, with the lower incisors meeting the upper dental pad. The upper lip is centrally divided and mobile to give more dexterity for feeding off certain plants.

The nose has two well-defined flaring nostrils. Darker pigmentation to the skin is preferred around the mouth and eyes giving them added protection to ultraviolet irradiation and the environment.

Major Faults:

1) Deafness in blue-eyed alpacas with lack of skin pigmentation and white fleece.
2) Gopher ears.
3) Superior and inferior prognathism.
4) Wry face.
5) Lump on the side of the face indicative of abscessing in the mouth.
6) Eyes: cataracts, entropy, ectropy, blindness.

Minor Faults:

1) A straight inside border or banana-type configuration of the ear indicating llama traits
2) Forward set ears.
3) Roman nose (llama tendency).
4) Narrow head
5) Muffled face in the Suri (fiber or hair impeding the alpaca's vision or retained on the adult face).
6) Retained or persistent deciduous teeth
7) Open faced with lack of fiber coverage over the face.
8) Lack of pigmentation around the lips and eyes

Height and Weight

The height at the withers of the adult alpaca is no less than 85cm (32") and the average weight of an adult alpaca is 60kg (140lbs).

Faults:

Small sized with less than 85cm (32") measurement at the withers. Oversized with llama characteristics.

Legs

The legs are supported by four two-toed feet, with each toe supporting a long toenail. They should be straight with the joints aligned to a perpendicular plumb line from the hip posteriorly and shoulder anteriorly. The shoulder blade is attached by muscular tissue to the thoracic cage but should move freely as the animal strides. A leathery padded membrane, which lessens the impact on the environment where they tread, protects the feet.

Major Faults:

1) Joints tracking medially or laterally to the vertical plum line.
2) Gaits associated with angular limb deformity such as winging, arcing, rope walking and throwing out of the front limbs where there is rotation at the joints of the front limb.

Genitalia (Female)

The genitalia of the female is protected internally and therefore not visible from the outside. However, the vaginal opening should be well covered by the tail, should not be too small and should be situated in a vertical rather than a horizontal plane.

Major Faults:

1) Too small of a vaginal opening.
2) Hermaphroditism.
3) Lack of any part of the reproductive system.

Minor Faults:

1) Horizontally situated pelvic floor.

2) Tipped up clitoris.

Genitalia (Male)

The most visible part of the male genitalia is the testicles that are situated and protected underneath the tail. The scrotum is well attached, relatively small and carries the testicles, which are relatively even in size.

The penis is also an external organ, which is situated under the belly between the rear legs. The normal size of fully developed testicles is: 4cm in length, 2.5cm in width in the adult male alpaca.

Major Faults:

1) Hermaphroditism.
2) Ectopic testicles (these testes are located outside the abdominal cavity under the skin, sometimes migrating down the leg).

Fleece - Huacaya

Huacaya alpacas produce a fine soft fiber that grows perpendicular to the skin. In the ideal Huacaya alpaca there is marked crimp formation as the fiber grows out of the skin. The hair follicles are situated close together in the skin, giving density to the fleece with groups of fibers bunching together to form defined staples. The following fiber characteristics are applicable to Huacaya fiber:

1) Fineness - this is the thickness of the fiber that is measured in microns. The finest fiber on the alpaca is found in the blanket area, however it is desirable to have fine fiber on the neck, belly, legs and topknot. Fineness is important for both commercial processor and the fiber grower since premium prices are paid for fine fiber and fine fiber translates into fine end products. Crimp is also related to fineness and it is desirable too to have a high number of waves per cm. or inch.

2) Density - is the number of fibers per square measurement of skin. Density is associated with fleece weight since the more fibers per square unit measurement, the more fleece will be grown and the heavier the fleece. A dense crimped fleece also acts as a barrier to dirt and weather.

3) Character -defined as strong crimp definition and staple formation.

4) Length of staple - is a very important factor in the amount of fleece shorn from the Huacaya alpaca. The more rapidly the length of staple that is grown the more weight of fleece there will be.

5) Brightness - is the amount of light that reflects from the fiber and is seen in the Huacaya. A brilliant appearance of the fleece is desirable.

6) Medulated fiber - is the coarse-microned fiber that grows in the lesser quality areas of the alpaca. Lack of medulated fiber in the prime or blanket area is desirable.

7) Uniformity of micron - processors require fleece of minimum variation in fiber diameter, therefore uniformity in fiber diameter is desirable across the blanket area of the alpaca. This also helps to eliminate fleece tenderness (fleece breakage) and prickle effect in the end product.

Faults:

1) Open fleece with no density
2) Harsh handle
3) Short staple length
4) Guard hair in the blanket
5) Lack of overall coverage
6) Tenderness and stress breaks
7) Felting and cotting

Fleece - Suri

The primary characteristics of the Suri fleece are its lock structure, high luster, silky handle and long staple length. The fleece falls close to the body, moves freely, and gives the Suri a flat-sided, lustrous appearance.

The locks can have a penciled ringlet formation, curling to the left or right, or a wave structure that forms from the skin of the alpaca. The fleece locking should begin from the forelock and continue uniformly down the neck, across the blanket and through the legs. The following fiber characteristics are applicable to Suri fiber:

1) Fineness - this is the thickness of the fiber, which is measured in microns. The finest fiber on the alpaca is found in the blanket area, however it is desirable to have fine fiber on the neck, belly, legs and topknot. Fineness is important for both commercial processor and the fiber

grower since premium prices are paid for fine fiber and fine fiber translated into fine end products.

2) Density - is the number of fibers per square measurement of skin. Density is associated with fleece weight since the more fibers per square unit measurement, the more fleece will be grown and the heavier the fleece.

3) Lock Structure - in the Suri lock structure is very important. The fibers group together to form ringlet type locks that turn to the right or to the left. Ideally, the lock should form a ringlet from the skin. However, it is common to find a lock structure that starts at the skin as a flat wave formation then continues out down the side of the alpaca in a ringlet.

4) Luster - is the sheen or shine that reflects from the fleece. This is a highly desirable trait in the Suri fleece and translates in the end product. The smooth flat structure of the outside cuticular layer of the individual fibers is responsible for this trait.

5) Length of staple - is a very important factor in the amount of fleece shorn from the Suri alpaca. The more length of staple that is grown the more weight of fleece there will be. A Suri will grow 60% longer fleece than Huacaya in one year's growth.

6) Medulation - there should be little or no evidence of medulated fibers in the fleece.

Faults:

1) Open fleece lacking lock definition.
2) Lack of density.
3) Crimp.
4) Harsh handle.
5) Short staple length.
6) Guard hair.
7) Lack of overall coverage.
8) Tenderness and stress breaks.
9) Felting and cotting.

Chapter 5. Alpaca Health and Breeding

Alpacas are highly adaptable animals. They have a hardy constitution cultivated over millennia living in the high, hostile Andes Mountains. It is rare for these animals to need more in the way of standard veterinary care than:

- castration
- worming
- annual inoculations
- Vitamin D supplementation
- toenail clipping

Because shearing of pets is a way to avoid heat stress it is technically a "healthcare" procedure, but obviously if the alpacas are kept as fiber producers, shearing occurs annually for reasons of profit. Preferably BEFORE you purchase your alpacas, you should locate a qualified veterinarian who will agree to care for your animals. Under the best circumstances, you will find a doctor with previous experience treating the animals.

Most "large animal" veterinarians who have treated sheep and goats can work with you to care for your alpacas, but it is imperative that the vet is agreeable to learning about the species and to consulting with other veterinarians who have expert knowledge in alpaca care.

It is to your benefit and to that of your animals that you cultivate a good working knowledge of alpaca healthcare needs. This will not only help you to make good decisions about the welfare of your animals, but also to control costs in this area of alpaca care.

At the very least, developing a working understanding of alpaca healthcare will help you to ask better questions.

I do not personally like to move forward with a healthcare procedure or treatment with any kind of animal until I am comfortable that I understand what is being done and why.

This is very much like the concept of "informed consent" in human healthcare. To truly be informed about the care your animals are receiving, you need to understand both the potential benefits **and** complications.

Body Scoring

As a basic evaluation of overall alpaca health, body scoring is a simple and fast method to determine the general state of the animal's wellbeing.

Hold or stand by the side of the alpaca.

Place your hand flat on the animal's back about 6" / 15 cm behind the withers.

Put your palm on the spine and your thumb on the ribs to one side of the backbone with your fingers to the other side. Press down firmly until you can feel the spine and ribs.

In healthy animals, you will feel a smooth line of flesh running from the spine to the ribs that is not indented (concave) or rounded (convex). Your thumb and forefingers will be in the shape of a "V."

If the spine protrudes upward and into your hand and the ribs are concave, the alpaca is overly thin.

If your thumb and fingers are relatively parallel and vertical to the animal, the alpaca is dangerously thin.

If your hand opens wide with bulging flesh between the spine and ribs, the alpaca is overweight. If your hand is horizontal and essentially flat, the animal is obese.

This simple evaluation can be performed daily in the morning or evening, and is easily done while you are feeding the alpacas.

Castration or Gelding

Many alpaca breeders castrate or "geld" males they do not intend to use for breeding purposes or that will be sold as pets when the animals are less than a year old. It's estimated that more than 80% of male alpacas are gelded, with only the top 10% used in breeding programs.

If your purchase a young male alpaca (18-24 months), the animal will likely already have been gelded, but be sure to ask. Since alpacas are herd animals that should not live alone, an intact male will have aggression issues due to the testosterone in his system.

At around three years of age, male alpacas develop "fighting teeth." These teeth grow into the lower jaw between the incisors and molars. They are very sharp and grow continuously, requiring annual trimming. Fighting males can seriously injure each other if this chore is not performed.

As an example of just how vicious an alpaca fight can be, and how seriously these animals take the matter of herd dominance, in the wild, a dominant male alpaca will sometimes use his fighting teeth at the end of a particularly violent struggle to castrate his opponent.

Worming

Like all livestock, alpacas become infested with parasites when they consume the eggs or larvae while grazing. If your local veterinarian has no previous experience with alpacas, the best course of action is to take a fecal sample to determine the correct deworming agent to use.

If no other animals are being kept on the land, alpacas can be wormed twice a year, typically in May and November. When other livestock, especially sheep, are kept in the same field, you may need to worm more often.

As with sheep, worming is accomplished via "drenching," which is the administration of a liquid de-wormer orally. Care must be taken, however, that the parasites present don't become resistant to the deworming agent.

Again, advice should be sought from your local veterinarian and other, more experienced alpaca farmers in your region about the frequency with which drenching should be administered and in what dosage.

But generally worm at 6 month intervals e.g. May and November. But if you have other livestock you'll need to worm more often (consult your vet)

I feel it's important to rotate worming products to help avoid building up resistance.

(Please note that if you are keeping alpacas in an area with a native population of whitetail deer, your animals will require monthly injections as protection against meningeal worms.)

Shearing

Obviously animals that are raised primarily for their fiber will be sheared on an annual basis. If you are keeping alpacas purely as pets, Huacaya alpacas must be sheared annually to guard against heat stress.

Suri alpacas can be sheared every other year. Shearing should be timed so that the animals have regrown at least 1 inch / 12.54 cm of fleece before the weather turns cold.

Teeth

The front teeth shouldn't protrude from the upper jaw as this can make grazing difficult. You'll need to trim the teeth back. Your vet is probably best as they can do this for you with clippers or dental wire. You may wish to consult a horse dentist who generally have a good understanding of this problem and can help reshape the whole jaw if required.

If you have a group of males you should trim the fighting teeth back to help stop them damaging other alpacas whilst they sort the pecking order out!

Feet

The toenails should not grow longer than the edge of the toe. If they do simply trim them back with sheep foot rot shears. Make sure you clear the dirt out so you can clearly see where the toe flesh is. The foot should be able to stand flat on the ground without twisting.

Vitamin D Supplementation

During the winter months, alpacas may require Vitamin D supplementation. Darker animals with dense fleece are even more susceptible to Vitamin D deficiency and to developing rickets. Again, however, the need for Vitamin D supplementation varies greatly by region and climate as well as by age of the animal.

Overdosing with Vitamin D can lead to organ failure. The supplement can be given as an injection or orally, but both forms should not be used at the same time.

Most vets are in agreement that the injectable Vitamin D is more readily absorbed and can be administered once every 60 days. The oral form is often given every 2 weeks.

A veterinarian should always be consulted before Vitamin D or any other kind of supplementation is used with your alpacas. Correct dosing with these products is essential.

Vaccination Protocols by Region

Working with your local veterinarian to determine the correct inoculations for your alpacas is critical. Disease and parasites VARY GREATLY by location and climate. These factors MUST be considered in developing a vaccination protocol for your animals.

In the UK, for instance, alpacas are vulnerable to the Bluetongue serotype viruses that are active on the continent as well as to local parasites like strongyle worms. Some areas of Britain also see a high prevalence of liver flukes.

In Britain, the recommended clostridial vaccinations are:

- Lambivac
- Covexin 10
- Heptavac-P Plus (includes Pasteurella)
- Ovivac or Ovivac-P

Heptavac is used to protect against:

- Lamb Dysentery
- Struck
- Pulpy Kidney
- Braxy
- Blackleg
- Tetanus
- Black Disease

Tetanus can develop all too easily from a simple cut. For this reason, annual CDT injections that protect against both tetanus and clostridial diseases are recommended.

Depending on your location, assume that your alpacas are vulnerable to all the diseases and parasites from which sheep can suffer.
In the U.S., recommended vaccinations include, but are not limited to:

IMRAB 3 (rabies)
CDT (tetanus and clostridium)
leptospirosis

These and other vaccinations used with alpacas in the U.S. are considered "off label" and have not been approved for use with these animals by the U.S. Department of Agriculture. Individual vets may have different opinions about which drugs work best.

(Please note that this information is provided as the basis for a conversation with your veterinarian about the vaccinations your animals will require and is not intended to be taken as a set protocol. I cannot stress strongly enough that required inoculations vary by region and should be dispensed according to expert veterinary advice.)

Toenail Clipping

Trimming your alpaca's toenails will be as easy or as hard as the animal decides to make it. This is a job that absolutely demands patience, and a willingness to concede defeat in any single session and finish the job on another day.

Standing on three legs while one foot is being held up for the trimming is an act of supreme trust on the part of the alpaca. Remember that you are dealing with a prey animal whose primary instinct when he feels threatened is to run.
In the wild, on the rocky slopes of their native South American mountainous range, alpacas keep their hooves worn down naturally. When they are pastured on soft ground, however, trimming is essential.

Animals with light colored toenails will need even more frequent trimmings as dark nails are harder and grow much slower. In some instance dark nails will only need to be trimmed annually at the time the animal is being sheared.

If the nails are not trimmed, they may cause the toe to twist painfully and pinch the pad. Long nails ultimately break off, leading the animal to go lame. It is even possible for a nail to overgrow to the point that it perforate the pad and causes a painful wound.

If you look at the underside of an alpaca's foot, you will see two toes and the soft pad. There are two nails.

Cradle the foot in your hand, with the underside up and visible.

Use a pair of garden pruning shears.*

Carefully trim the nails until they sit level with the bottom of the pad.

*There are many kind of clippers that will work well including those specifically designed to be used with sheep and goats. The important thing is that the implement be comfortable in your hand for maximum control and sharp enough to accomplish the trimming quickly and efficiently.

Conditions Common to Alpacas

All of the following conditions are common to alpacas, but like all health matters concerning these animals, are greatly affected by location. Also, this is not an all-inclusive list, but rather an overview of conditions commonly associated with alpacas.

Rickets or Vitamin D Deficiency

Alpacas of less than 2 years of age as well as females who are pregnant or nursing can be susceptible to rickets as a result of Vitamin D deficiency. This is also true of animals with especially thick fleece.

During the winter months the lower levels of sunlight cause an abnormal ratio of calcium to phosphate, which affects bone growth. Demineralization of the long bones, called osteomalacia, accompanies rickets and presents with a painful series of symptoms including:

a hunched posture
obvious discomfort when moving
walking slowly with legs splayed
the appearance of leaning backward while walking

An affected animal will lag behind the rest of the flock and spend most of its time in the kush or resting position with the legs tucked under the body.

Treatment for rickets includes injections of Vitamin D and phosphorous supplements, but care must be taken not to overdose the alpaca with toxic levels. Consultation with a knowledgeable veterinarian is essential.

Tuberculosis

Alpacas have little if any resistance to tuberculosis and are extremely vulnerable to the disease. This susceptibility is complicated by the fact that there is no reliable TB test that can be used. The skin test used widely with cattle detects only about 20% of cases in alpacas and the blood test is equally unreliable and often gives false positives.
Signs of tuberculosis in alpacas include:

- lethargy
- self-isolation from the group
- weight loss (often sudden)
- coughing

If the disease develops in the thoracic and abdominal cavities there may be no visible signs. TB often progresses so rapidly that the animals are simply discovered dead in the pasture for no apparent reason.

Under these circumstances, it's important that a vet examine the body to determine if TB is present. Interestingly, however, alpacas do not then seem to transmit the disease among themselves, but rather to contract it from other infected livestock, usually cattle. TB can also be transmitted from wildlife to alpacas. In the UK, for instance, tuberculosis is present in Shropshire badgers.

These animals come into the pasture to forage on animal droppings and can infect alpacas grazing in the area. Badgers can only be kept out of fields by burying wire three feet / 1 meter into the ground on the fenced perimeter.

Check with your local alpaca association to see if there is a program for testing and reporting cases of tuberculosis.

IMPORTANT NOTE: Tuberculosis is a zoonotic disease and can be transmitted from animal to humans.

Dietary Poisoning

All grazing animals can be inadvertently poisoned by plants with which they come into contact in the pasture. This is also true of garden plants to which alpacas may be exposed on smaller farms adjacent to planted yards. Plants known to be poisonous to alpacas include, but are not limited to:

- nightshade
- lilies
- azaleas
- solanums
- inkweed
- foxglove
- oleander
- hemlock
- willow weed
- tutu (toot)
- ragwort
- ngaio
- datura
- mallow
- Jerusalem cherry
- yew
- buttercup
- laurel
- irises
- macrocarpa
- bracken fern
- hellebores
- daffodils

If you suspect that your alpaca has ingested a poisonous plant, immediately seek the assistance of a qualified veterinarian.

Facial Eczema

Facial eczema in livestock is caused by a mycotoxin in the pasture. The spores of various types of fungus contain sporidesmin, a toxic chemical that damages the liver, preventing the normal breakdown of metabolic and digestive toxins in the bloodstream.

As these toxins build up, the compounds that leach into the skin react to sunlight. Clinical symptoms include:

1) skin irritation
2) crusting and oozing of the ears and nose

3) decreased growth rates in young animals
4) spontaneous abortions
Since alpacas hide signs of illness, liver disease is often not discovered until the animal has succumbed to a sudden death and a liver biopsy is performed.

Ryegrass Staggers

In areas where perennial ryegrass is popular, alpacas can be exposed to the endophyte fungus **Acremonium lilii**. When ingested, the mycotixns produced by the fungus attack the brain and central nervous system causing "ryegrass staggers."

Symptoms of the condition include tremors of the head and neck and an unstable gait (ataxia). If left untreated, the alpaca will collapse and die. Susceptibility seems to have a genetic component, and ryegrass staggers are seen more frequently in the summer and autumn. Hay cut from an infected pasture remains toxic, however, so animals can be symptomatic at any time.

If treated at an early stage with Mycosorb or Biomass in combination with good quality lucerne hay and fresh water, the alpaca will recover within a few weeks.

Bovine Viral Diarrhea (BVD)

Bovine viral diarrhea is a disease that has affected alpacas in North America since 2001. It is acute and short term, and if the alpacas are healthy, their robust immune system is usually capable of eradicating the illness quickly. However, if the virus is contracted by a pregnant female, the chances that she will abort the fetus are high. If the baby lives, it may well be infected with BVD persistently and be a carrier of the virus.

Overview of Alpaca Breeding

Obviously the subject of alpaca breeding can be addressed from the perspective of a business.

Mating

Alpaca females only ovulate during the act of mating, conceiving shortly afterwards, which makes artificial insemination difficult. This type of reproduction is called "induced ovulation" and is stimulated both by the motion of the male and by the "orgling" noise he makes.

A young female alpaca is ready to be placed with a stud male when she is 14 months of age, or when she has attained 60 % of her mother's weight.

Male alpacas are ready to breed when they are 2-3 years of age, although some are capable of mating as young as nine months.

The selection of the stud male is the critical decision in creating a mating pair as the male has the greatest influence on the quality of the offspring. This why only about 10% of alpaca males are left intact to be herdsires. Most males are gelded and kept for their fiber or sold as pets.

During copulation, the female sits for the male in the kush position. He mounts her from behind. (Females that are not receptive refuse to sit and will often spit at the males to reject their advances.) Because male alpacas are dribble ejaculators, mating may last as long as 45 minutes.

Do not be alarmed if there is evidence of blood at the completion of mating, especially if the female alpaca is being bred for the first time.

Gestation and Birth

The average period of gestation is 345 days, but varies from 330 to 370 days. The best time of year for the young, called cria, to be born is late spring into early summer. If, however, the correct shelters and facilities are in place, many breeders plan births from March through October.

Typically alpaca births occur during the middle of the day and are free of any trouble. The cria should be 12-20 pounds / 5.4-9 kg at birth and within 2-3 hours will be on their feet and nursing. Mothers are quite protective and will not wean their babies for 5-6 months.

Planning Matings

Even if a female is nursing her cria, she can still be re-mated 2-6 weeks after giving birth. This means that in planned breeding programs, maintaining multiple pastures to separate the breeding animals is essential.

For this reason, pen mating is often the best method. This requires a space 10-14 feet / 3.04-4.26 meters gated on one side. In good weather, this is easily created with portable fencing in a pasture. The pen sides should be

4-5 feet / 1.2-1.5 meters high. In pasture mating, it's best to choose an area new to both animals.

Confirming Ovulation

Seven days after the initial mating, the pair should be re-introduced. If the female refuses to sit for the male, the chances are quite good that she has indeed ovulated and conceived. Repeat this process at days 14, 21, and 28 to confirm the outcome. (Large breeding operations will test via ultrasound.)

General health

For the most part, alpacas are very healthy animals with a robust constitution. However, there are still some basic precautions that you must take to maintain their health, in addition to supplementing their diet for potential mineral deficiencies.

The regular maintenance routine consists of two main vaccinations, rabies and CDT (Clostridium, Diphtheria, Tetanus), and parasite control. You will save a considerable amount of money if you learn to do your own routine shots. Your veterinarian or an experience alpaca breeder should be happy to show you how to do both sub-Q (subcutaneous) and IM (intramuscular) injections.

The rabies is an annual vaccination, requiring a vet for certification. CDT is given a couple days after birth, a booster at two months and six months and then annually thereafter. Routine vaccinations are extremely important and should not be missed unless the animal is under specialized care from the vet.

Year-round internal parasite (worms) monitoring is an absolute necessity. No deworming injectable or oral product is 100% effective at treating all parasites. This makes it especially important to first identify the parasites present on your farm and then to treat each infected alpaca at the proper dose based on the alpaca's weight.

As confirmation that you are dosing the animals effectively, it is useful to carry out fecal tests on a regular basis. Most veterinary clinics can perform these services. Testing is also easily accomplished by the alpaca owner by investing in a small microscope (used ones are readily available) and a kit that is readily available from veterinary suppliers and other stores.

In the eastern half of the United States, one of the main problems is the infiltration of meningeal worms. This parasite is transmitted via slugs, and ticks from white-tailed deer, causing serious problems if your animals become infected. The larvae can cause a severe reaction in the spinal chord that interferes with nerve impulses.

Some alpaca farmers regularly administer deworming medications year-round as a preventative. They may have done this for years and feel good about their efforts. New research has shown that the problem with this approach is that the common deworming medications are less than effective for certain types of worms and may allow them to thrive for years unknown to the owner. The absolute best method is to first Identify and then treat.

Your local farmer's cooperative or agricultural store will stock the syringes, needles, and vaccines that you need. They can also advise you on safe disposal of used needles.

Teeth and toenails

Your alpacas will also need to have their teeth and toenails checked regularly. It is important that the lower teeth meet the dental pad at the top, and do not under- or over-shoot. If they are growing too long, they can be filed or cut back using a DremelTM tool with a rotary grinding disk or an OB cutting wire. Depending on the nature of your animal, they may need to be sedated. Your vet can provide some assistance with the whole teeth trimming procedure. If you have older males, their fighting teeth will grow after 2 or 3 years. These are sharp teeth that grown on the side of the jaw. They will need to be cut back; otherwise they can do serious damage when play fighting with other males.

The toenail trimming is an easy task - once you have gotten the alpaca to stand still. There are many good books that illustrate how to trim the nails properly. Consult one of these before attempting to cut them yourself, or have the seller demonstrate the proper procedure and tools. Often, toenails are trimmed while shearing the animal. This way the animal is fully restrained and the trimming can be done easily.

Nutrition

Few new alpaca owners (or even many experienced ones) possess previous experience in providing balanced nutrition for birthing herds of animals. This is why knowledge of alpaca nutrition is essential to maintaining a healthy herd. A well know camelid veterinarian, Dr. Norm Evans, states it this way, "Anyone can feed, but nutrition requires effort". We must realize that camelids, people, and every other species have different nutritional needs based on their daily activity, size and use. Alpacas that are kept relatively parasite free can survive nicely on many diets. The alpaca body is made up of nearly 40 vitamins and minerals in unique balance. Utilized nutrients must be replaced; otherwise, imbalances and deficiencies will occur.

Another respected camelid veterinarian, Dr. David Anderson, notes that "too often, nutrition is equated with feed alone." He believes little thought may be applied to the type of feed (grain, pellets, crumbles, hay, grass, water), how it is fed (individual feeders, bulk feeders, free choice troughs), how it is stored, the animals' access to the feed (feed hierarchy), and the animals' utilization of the feed (fine-ground grain vs. high-fiber roughage). Alpacas are particularly susceptible to these factors because their social structure and the lack of livestock experience of many alpaca owners.

Indeed, most alpacas enjoy and can exist on many different foods, but just like humans, much of what they eat and the quantity consumed can cause health problems over time. If we want them to stay healthy and perform at maximum efficiency, we need to provide nutrition that addresses their needs. Nutrients depleted or utilized for growth, breeding, gestation, or lactation and not present in the forage must be provided for or replaced.

As you can see, there is much alpaca owners should know about feeding and nutrition. Complete coverage of this topic would take many pages and is certainly outside the scope of this report. The bibliography contains several good resources for more information on this topic. I will close this section with Dr. Evans eight main points of alpaca nutrition;

1) Understand the alpaca's use (fiber only or breeding) and nutritional needs base on use.

2) Know where the nutrients come from (water, hay, pasture, vitamins, minerals, supplements).

3) Balance the nutrients deficient in the tested forage.

4) Frame score and body score all adults and supplement accordingly.

5) Weigh, keep records, and be aware of seasonal gains and losses.

6) Remove human error when feeding; weigh the animals feed intake for 7 days.

7) Always supplement per feed tag recommendations to avoid toxic levels of copper, selenium, etc.

8) Always let new hay cure 4-6 weeks prior to feeding.

Conditioning

In the alpacas' natural environment, it is virtually impossible for them to overeat and get fat. Unfortunately, that is not the case in North America. Many of the animals that you see on your farm visits may well be over-conditioned. As well as the obvious risk that this poses to health, it can also lead to lower reproductive capability, and birthing problems.

To prevent your animals from slowly creeping up in weight, routinely of weigh them on a monthly basis. You should also ask the breeder who supplies your alpacas to show you how to carry out body score checks. This basically consists of feeling the animal near the spine, between the withers and the hips, and assessing the amount of fat there.

The score is reported on a scale of either 1 to 5, or 1 to 10, when discussing scores with other people; make sure that you are on the same scale. In either case, the lower score represents being seriously underweight, and the higher one, seriously obese. You obviously want to be in the middle, at either 3 or 5, depending on the scale.

Chapter 6. Frequently Asked Questions

While it is necessary to read the entire text to get an understanding of both alpacas and the alpaca industry, the following are some of the questions I am asked most frequently about the animals and their fiber.

What is an alpaca?

Alpacas are "camelids" indigenous to South America. They are closely related to llamas, and less so to Asian and African camels.

These docile herbivores produce exceptionally high quality textile fiber, and their cultivation for this purpose on a worldwide basis has been steadily growing since the 1980s.

What is a Suri alpaca?

Suri alpacas have unique fiber characteristics different from Huacaya alpacas. Their fiber is extremely fine and soft, hanging in long, lustrous locks with no crimping. It grows parallel to the body and may be either flat or twisted.

Suri fiber is highly sought after in the fashion industry and by spinners and weavers. It is very like cashmere, with a silky touch. Though lightweight, it is exceptionally warm and durable and can easily be blended with wool and silk. This type of alpaca is very rare, however. As an example, sufis make up only about 10 % of all the alpacas present in North America.

What is a Huacaya alpaca?

The fiber of a Huacaya alpaca is wooly in appearance, dense, and crimped. The resulting look on the animal itself is that of a huggable teddy bear. In North America, about 90% of all alpacas are Huacayas. Their fiber is fine and highly prized.

What is the difference between alpacas and llamas?

One of the easiest ways for the newcomer to this industry to tell an alpaca and a llama apart is to look at the ears. Alpacas are physically smaller than llamas, but their ears are straight while llamas have curved ears that look rather like bananas. In terms of the fiber, the coat of a llama is interspersed with coarser guard hairs that must be removed during processing, while alpaca fiber is very fine and soft.

Behaviorally, llamas are much more aggressive and are often used as guard animals for grazing herds of sheep and even alpacas themselves.

Do alpacas make good pets?

Although alpacas are docile and social, their primary reaction to everything in their environment stems from their existence as prey animals. In general, they are wary of humans.

They do not like to be grabbed, and there are areas of the body (feet, lower legs, and abdomen) where they do not like to be touched. If handled well, they will interact peacefully with humans, but they won't come when they are called like dogs or cats, nor do they really like much in the way of petting. Some individuals are however, more affectionate than others.

Are alpacas smart?

Yes, alpacas are highly intelligent and adaptable. They have inquisitive and curious natures, but do follow the dominant herd members. This does not, however, prevent them from learning new tasks quickly and being cooperative with their handlers. Although not necessarily making good "pets," per se, they do seem to enjoy their interaction with humans and some individuals can be quite affectionate.

Do alpacas spit like camels?

Alpacas do have the ability to bring up acidic solid material from their stomachs, which they will spit at one another, but rarely at humans. This behavior is most often seen during feeding times or other situations where dominance comes into play. It is not a harmful behavior, and doesn't escalate into more serious confrontations.

What do alpacas eat?

Alpacas are grazing herbivores, existing primarily on a diet of grasses. They do not, however, pull the grass up by the roots, so the pastures on which they are placed will renew if the herd is rotated regularly.

They do best on low protein grasses. If fed higher protein forage like alfalfa or clover, alpacas may experience health problems and the quality of their fleece will suffer.

What kind of shelter do alpacas need?

Sheltering alpacas from the elements is strictly determined by location. In areas where winter temperatures fall below freezing and heavy snowfall is the norm, a three-sided shelter will protect the animals from the elements.

In areas with high summer heat and a lot of humidity, the same three-sided type shelter can be used to provide shade, but an additional means of cooling (like the use of sprinklers in the pasture) will be needed. Put up a permitter fence in keeping with the degree of security necessary to protect the alpacas from the types of predators indigenous to your area.

How large a pasture will I need for my alpacas?

The amount of pasture you will need for your alpacas will depend on the ability of the land to produce quality grass in relation to climate and precipitation. In general, however, an acre / 0.4 hectare of good quality pasture will support approximately 5-10 alpacas.

What is the lifespan of an alpaca?

The expected lifespan of an alpaca is 15-20 years.
How to Raise Alpacas

After buying the alpacas, the first step in raising them is obtaining a DBA (Doing Business As) certificate. This is usually obtained from the office of the town clerk. If your objective is to rear the alpacas as a business where you can sell the alpacas themselves, their end products or their fleece, then you need to go further and obtain a license from the state. Finally, if you are starting the alpaca business with a large number of stocks, then you need to obtain an agricultural permit as well. Once you have all the necessary permits, you are good to go.

Feeding

The good thing about alpacas is that they are very economical with food. Feeding an average alpaca costs about the same as feeding a farm dog. Being cud chewers, they mostly feed on pasture. They are, however, also browsers. That means that they can also comfortably feed on bushes and shrubs.

Grazing the alpacas is not enough for them. It is important that you also buy them hay. Take care to ensure that the hay bought is healthy and grown in conditions suitable for feeding alpaca. That means that it should not have any moldy or musty smell and should be stored under cover when bought. In addition to that, it shouldn't be either dusty or look bleached. Good hay is hay that is green and is visibly healthy.

When feeding them, it's also important that you ensure the alpacas get all the minerals required by their body. The forage available in the US usually lacks some of the critical minerals required by alpacas. The alpacas are natives of South America and therefore there are so many minerals their bodies are used to obtaining naturally there that are not readily available in the US. It is therefore critical that you identify the minerals that are crucial but which are lacking in the forage. Commercial food mixes for alpacas have lots of these needed minerals as well as vitamins. You should therefore buy them in substantial quantities to complement their normal food.

It is also not advisable to suddenly change the diet of the alpacas after arrival. Rather, keep the change gradual over a period of around two months. In this way, you prevent the alpaca from developing health complications.

Alpacas need a lot of water. The exact quantities differ depending on the seasons. During winter, their water intake is usually less than in summer. This is because there is not much loss of water from their bodies in the winter temperatures. This is however not the case during summer. Then, they lose a lot of water from their bodies. As a result, they have to take a lot of water to replace the lost water. At this time they may take as much as four liters per day. It is therefore important that water is available to them at all times especially during summer.

Shearing

The coat has to be sheared regularly. It is recommended that the shearing be done at least once every year. This should be done before that period of the year when your area is too hot near to summer. At this time, the coat does not play any crucial role for the protection of the alpaca since there is no cold to be protected from. Leaving the coat during the summer is likely to lead to heat stress which may bring health complications. When shearing, the whole body is sheared.

Temperatures

Keep alpacas where the temperatures are not too high. High temperatures and humidity cause alpacas to develop heat stress and a range of other illnesses. A heat index is used to determine the acceptable level of heat and humidity that an alpaca can survive in. This is done by adding the temperature and the percentage of humidity. The temperature taken is in farads. A heat index of 120 to 180 is taken as being acceptable. A heat index of above 180 is unsuitable for the raising of alpacas.

When the heat gets high the alpaca starts showing signs of heat stress. These include nasal flaring, increased breathing and heart rate, dullness, trembling and drooling. Whenever these signs occur, you should cool the alpaca with water. In cooling it using this method, ensure that you soak the alpaca in the water rather than just pouring some water on the body's surface. In addition you should make it drink a lot of water. In this way it will have enough water to cool the body correctly.

Find a veterinarian

It is critical that you find a veterinarian near you with enough knowledge of alpacas. This is because there are so many things about the health of an alpaca that you might not know yourself. Having a veterinarian will help you carry out checkups and routine shots as well as other treatments at the right times, which will be advised by the vet. As you gain experience in alpaca rearing, you should learn some of these skills. This will save you the cost of having to consult a veterinarian every now and then. In addition, it will also ensure that you are able to meet emergencies effectively.

Having to rely on a veterinarian to help you in case of emergencies is not entirely advisable. There is always the possibility that an emergency might occur when a vet is not available so learning about the breed is vital. In such a scenario, you face the risk of losing your alpaca.

Having some skills of your own is therefore a big plus in the raising of alpacas. These skills can be obtained from a trained veterinarian or an experienced alpaca farmer. Even before getting some informal lessons, it pays to spend some time with the alpacas. This will help you familiarize yourself with them and understand some fine details about them that will definitely go a long way in helping to better take care of them.

Treatment

Alpacas can be easily killed by parasites if their health is not well taken care of. To prevent this from occurring fecal testing should be done on the alpacas periodically. This will help you have timely treatment for parasites and worms.

Getting Insurance coverage

Like all businesses, raising alpaca has its own share of risks. To ensure that the occurrence of these risks does not significantly destabilize your business, it is important that you get insurance coverage for various aspects of alpaca farming. The most important risk is the lives of the alpacas themselves.

If you have enough money at your disposal you may insure all the alpacas on the farm. However if there isn't much money, then make sure you insure the most valuable alpacas. These are the female alpacas that are responsible for producing offspring. As long as these are insured, you are sure of getting a replacement within a very short period of time.

Apart from the alpacas, there are a number of other things that need to be insured on the farm. These include the building coverage as well as the equipment used on the farm in the rearing of alpacas.

Why Should You Raise Alpaca?

Change in lifestyle

Rapid urbanization, especially in developed countries, has alienated many people. These people can't just feel uncomfortable with the hustle and bustle of urban life. The constant noise and crowds put a lot of pressure on them. It is for this reason they long for a relaxed environment where they can live quietly and in peace. A rural setting is the best place to guarantee such an environment.

However, the fact that there are very few money-making opportunities in rural areas makes such a choice difficult to make for people who might have such yearnings. Alpaca farming solves this problem. It not only offers you a chance to live a quiet, peaceful rural life away from the hustle and bustle of urban life but also gives you a chance to make money. With this money, you can comfortably live your dream without fear of going broke.

Low Maintenance Second Business

Raising alpacas can provide a very lucrative part time business. This is because raising alpacas do not require much effort and time. If you have another business already in place, an alpaca business can be a great second business. You will be sure that it will not eat away much time from your main business while providing you a handsome extra income. Those with jobs who are not comfortable with their income can also significantly increase their income through an alpaca business.

The good thing about it is that you will not have to resign from your daily job since the little free time available to you on a daily business will enable you to comfortably raise the alpacas.

Enjoy animal companionship

Alpacas provide great company to human beings of all ages. Their softness, colorfulness and gentleness make them even great companions for children. Others have found the alpacas humming sound is a great stress reliever. After a long day's work or a stressful event, listening to the alpacas humming is very soothing and produces a great background to relaxation.

The fact that alpacas have only teeth at the bottom side of their mouth makes it impossible for them to bite you. For this reason they are pretty harmless to be around. You can play with them for as long as you wish without fearing any harm. If you are looking for a pet, you should consider having alpacas.

Making profit and tax deductions

Most farmers who engage in raising alpacas do so in order to make money. Indeed alpaca farming is a money-making activity. Most of the farmers who raise alpacas for profit get their money from the breeding business which is quite lucrative. The selling of fiber is also profitable. Many of the top fashion designers use fiber from alpacas. This is because it is very high quality.

Unfortunately, this aspect of the alpaca industry is yet to fully develop. It has however shown a lot of potential of developing in the future. Until then, alpaca breeding is going to remain the biggest money-maker for alpaca farmers.

In addition to the profits it provides, alpaca farming also qualifies breeders for handsome tax deductions and advantages if the alpacas are raised actively for profit. All expenses incurred in raising the alpacas are usually written off against the income. The expenses include those incurred in taking care of the alpacas like paying veterinarian fees, fertilizer, food and treatment. Also treated as expenses is the tangible property that depreciates in value over time. These include barns, the breeding stock and fences. Based on these expenses, you can also have your cash flow sheltered from taxes.

A passive owner might not enjoy all of these tax advantages but will still have some of the advantages. These include the direct cost of caring for the alpacas and the breeding stock itself being written off in case of losses.

Another tax advantage offered is the tax deferred wealth-building. In this arrangement, you do not have to pay income tax on every alpaca that you buy. Rather, you are allowed to buy as many as you can and grow the herd to whichever number you feel like having without having to pay income tax. The tax is only paid after you have sold all your herd of alpacas.

For you to have all these tax advantages, you need to have your books up to date to show that you are a hands-on farmer. Those who raise alpacas as a hobby cannot qualify for this tax deduction and other advantages. The IRS considers a for-profit farmer as one who has recorded making some profit in at least three of the previous five years. Included is the current year. If your alpaca business does not meet this threshold, then you will not be considered as a for-profit business. As such, you will not be able to qualify for the tax advantages and deductions described above.

Easy to raise

Alpacas are some of the easiest animals to raise today. It is very easy to handle them. Their relative small size and gentleness makes them quite easy to deal with by almost anyone. Apart from the ease of handling them, their food is also very cheap. Being grazers and browsers at the same time, they can easily find food anywhere. All that is required is buying more hay to compliment the nutrients found in the pastures.

As for shelter, they can even survive without a barn. Shade is only required to prevent them from suffering from heat stress and winds. In addition alpacas only require a relatively small piece of land to be comfortably raised. An acre of land can accommodate up to ten alpacas. If you do not have a piece of land you can still raise alpacas. This is achieved through letting your alpacas be handled by a veteran breeder as you board with him and learn the ins and outs of alpaca farming. It is this general ease of raising the alpacas that makes alpaca farming quite attractive to many people.

Preparing for Shearing

It's that time again and the shearer is coming in a few days and you have to prepare for the visit.

It's important that the area you have chosen for shearing is scrupulously clean. This is of course for two reasons – firstly you want to ensure that should your animal get cut during shearing, that he/she doesn't run the risk of getting an infection. Secondly you need to ensure that there is no organic matter or dust lying around that could cling onto your fleeces. The dust in the fleece could cause the shearer a problem by blunting his tools, and you want to avoid having to arduously remove organic matter from the fleeces before you pack them!

If the weather forecast is good then you have no problem. But if there is a risk of rain then you need to bring your animals into a dry area before it rains. Your shearer may refuse to shear them if they are wet, for it could damage his tools, but from your fleece point of view, you really don't want a wet fleece that will have to be dried before you can pack it away. There are many methods of shearing and you need to liaise with your shearer as to how he needs the area set up before he arrives.

Some shearers insist on all the alpacas being in the vicinity whilst some will fetch them from the fields for you. Personally I like to bring them in before the shearer arrives so that the whole operation can be conducted as soon as possible. Alpacas are sensitive animals and don't like to be restrained in an area for too long. They seem to work on the 100th Monkey Syndrome and can pass the message to each other that they are about to have an experience that they probably won't enjoy.

Do make sure that your shearer is experienced with Alpacas. They are not sheep, can't be manhandled like sheep, and shouldn't be shorn like sheep! I heard a story of an Alpaca shearer who was self-taught – whilst he did restrain the animal securely he sheared them from hind foot across the blanket to the front foot. As he sheared his helper removed bits of the fleece, mixing blanket with legs and the owners just ended up with a pile of handfuls of fleece. The result was of course a ruined fleece, for no beautiful blanket to admire and a complete mix of blanket and legs. The animal though was a lot cooler so there was some sort of result. Any good shearer will remove the blanket for you in virtually one piece so that you can pack it straight away. The remaining part of the fleece can then be easily collected and stored separately.

If you have helpers available this is a good time to skirt the blanket. Lay it out on a flat surface with the cut side facing up. This should be done on a wire mesh table (skirting table) that allows debris to fall from the fleece. Spend a little time looking over the edges of the fleece and remove debris and any obvious guard hairs (seen as straight coarse hairs), which would devalue the fleece's consistency. Fold the sides of the fleece into the middle and roll the fleece up gently.

How you store your fleece is a matter of personal choice. But you need to make sure that the fleeces are dry before storage. A wet fleece will eventually grow mould and taint the entire fleece making it completely unusable. We use paper feed bags or potato sacks that have several layers, for storage. This way the blanket goes in, the layer is folded over the fleece and then the remaining fleece is placed in and the next layer folded over it.

If your shearer allows you the time, it is a great opportunity to weigh your blanket and the separated fleece and write it on the outside of the bag for future use. If you are lucky you will have several helpers on hand, who could do this for you.

Incidentally, shearing time is a great time to have the teeth and toes dealt with, and to do any injections or drenching. Most shearers offer to do the teeth and toes and some to even do the injections for you. It does of course sometimes add to the shearing cost, but it does make life a lot easier when the Alpaca is in a restrained position.

If you are planning on having your fibre evaluated for micron count (histogram) then you should tell your shearer before he starts. He will take a small sample from the mid-side of the alpaca, which you then need to place in a ziplock bag to go off to your provider to make the appropriate measurements and send you a report.

About Fibre

It is outside the remit of this book to delve into histogram reports, but suffice it to say that the report only reveals the findings of that piece of fleece on that day. If the sample is taken incorrectly (i.e. not close to the skin) it will give an inaccurate result. As the animal gets older, one can expect the micron count to increase.

So what purpose does the micron count serve? Whilst it is a useful tool for determining the health of your alpaca, it is also used for genetic improvement. The fleece sample when analysed, records, amongst other things, the diameter of the fibres and this is expressed in microns (one millionth of a metre, or one thousandth of a millimetre).

It is used by many to determine what usage will be made of the fleece, but this differs throughout the Alpaca Community and between mill spinners and hand spinners.

Microns and the Buyer

Many businesses will buy your fleeces either to sell on to someone else, or to add to their own fleeces for mill processing. In these instances it is most likely that you will be paid according to the microns. However, on the whole the buyer will be able to identify the micron so it isn't always necessary for you to have the fibre tested beforehand. However you should check with them first.

Comparatively, in sheep, I understand that in the UK the fleeces are sold as a whole at a fixed price by breed, to the British Wool Marketing Board. Therefore there is no need for micron testing to determine the price of the sheep fleece.

The usage of the micron value is one that is easily recognised by those who have alpacas. However, from my own experience, the general public would appear to be totally unaware of it. They therefore view the alpaca fleece or product by how soft it feels/looks, and what colour it is. As they don't know about microns, they rarely, if ever, ask.

Certainly, in all the years that I have sold fleeces and products, I have only once been asked what the micron value was. I confirmed that I had not had the fleece tested and therefore didn't know. The buyer however purchased the fleece from the photograph included in the advertisement, and went on to order different colour fleeces.

It is true to say that if you peruse some of the advertisements offering fleeces for sale, very rarely do you see the micron referred to.

So how do you know what the best use of the fibre is? For me, the best analogy is human hair. As a baby we have very fine downy hair which will not hold a plait. As we grow older the hair thickens but can still be a bit wispy. It will hold a plait but not tightly. The older we get and the hair becomes thicker and denser, the more likely it is that we can plait the hair and it will hold exactly how we plaited it. Past a certain age it gets less dense and the plait gets thinner.

Experienced hand and mill spinners know from the look and feel of the fleece exactly what it can be used for – even if they have only seen a photograph.

Spinning Into Yarn

Hand Spinning - By the time we decided to actually do something with the fleece we had two years supply and additional fleeces donated by friends (guess they didn't know what to do with it!).

I decided to learn how to spin and found a suitable class through a Spinners Guild. I made sure that my tutor was fully experienced and compassionate, for I was absolutely clueless about fibre of any description.
After the first day I was eager to throw the spinning wheel out of the window, and not return for a second class. But the tutor was compassionate (remember that was one of the qualifications I sought) and loaned me a spinning wheel to practice on at home. In the quietness of the house and without competition from other members of the group who were doing much better than I, it all became much easier. The determination and interest that I started with returned and having mastered the basic skill, I was able to sail through the rest of the course with ease.

That course taught me about skirting and washing sheep fleeces, carding (more about that later) working with wool, cotton, silk, recycled bottle tops, hemp, and even dog hair. I learned the difference between long draw and short draw and how to ply the yarn. I also learned about drop spindling but I have to admit that I wasn't very good at that. Luckily, at my request, we also played with an alpaca fleece that I proudly took in to class.

As an aside you don't have to wash alpaca fleece which is going to be spun as it contains no lanolin. It will be washed after it is plied and made into a skein, in order to set the spinning.

If you think you would like to learn to spin then please do find someone from a Guild. At the one I used they would loan any equipment for you to use at home, so the only expense was enrolling for the class. The tutor provided all the materials and thankfully tea and coffee.

Mill Spinning – Armed with the newly gleaned knowledge I had gained from the Hand Spinning class, we sought out a local mill. Whilst there are many mills around that you can just send your fleeces to, as we were novices we wanted to have a one-to-one chat with the processor. This Mill also had a shop full of things that had been woven from sheep and alpaca and sometimes a mixture of both. There were scarves, cushions, throws, and garments, so we got lots of ideas as well as indication of price for a completed item.

We learned that you cannot use wool spun for weaving, to actually knit with, for it knits on the slant. I didn't believe him so tried it for myself and it was true. But, you can use yarn spun for knitting, also for weaving with no problem. Inspired by all the things in the shop, we decided that I would learn to weave and therefore we definitely needed the yarn spun for knitting. (Rather than the other way round).

For weaving I had learned from the spinning class that we would need a 2 fold yarn (2 ply), but we also knew that not many knitters would use a 2ply although those who did crochet would. So, we also agreed to have 4ply. As alpaca fleece is much warmer than sheep, we decided against Double Knit.

We were disappointed to learn though that the finished product wouldn't be ready for several months and this seems to be true of all Mills. So you do need to get your fleeces to your chosen Mill as soon as possible.
The Mill gave us lots of choices, just washed and dried fibre, carded fibre, picked fibre (just all pulled apart by machine – great for stuffing), coned yarn, hanks (skeins) or balls.

As we were on a limited budget we chose the coned yarn. We have lived to regret it though sometimes, because winding from a cone into a ball even with equipment does take up time. But the upside is that it's easy to wind into skeins for dyeing into pretty colours.

Dyeing Fibre

Learning to hand dye became a necessary option for us. Whilst the Mill offered to have the yarn professionally dyed for us, this seemed an unnecessary expense.
Most of our fleeces were white but we do have many coloured alpacas too. We decided that we would hand dye some of the white and simply see what happened.
Hand dyeing is exciting, for you are never absolutely certain of the exact colour that will result. It does take quite a lot of time though for the whole process, but it is really worthwhile.

There are many types of dyes, and alpaca fibre takes up the dye quite well. For muted colours we have used natural dyes. For brighter colours we have used acid dyes. Brighter colour still is achieved by using Fibre Reactive dyes.

I don't intend in this book to go into the methods of dyeing. There are many good books already written on the subject as well as hoards of Youtube videos. My favourite book is, Color in Spinning by Deb Menz. It gives you guidance on spinning, dyeing, carding, and even items to make as well as lots of colour charts. It truly is a fantastic Spinners and Dyers Bible and one that I would not want to part with. There are, however, many other books to choose from – I just happen to think that this one covers most of the things I need to know.

Whilst you can dye your fleece before making into yarn, we were advised by the Mill we used that if we did that, they wouldn't be able to spin it for us – apparently it would damage their machines. But that was not a problem for we wanted to only dye part of our white fleeces once they had been made into beautiful yarn.

If, however, you are going to hand-spin then dyeing raw fibre isn't a problem. If you go in this direction then you can make beautiful textured yarns by blending several colours together in different formats.
But now that we had learned to dye we ventured into learning to weave for this would add another way of selling the end results of our fibre.

Weaving

Taking up this additional craft was just, for us, natural progression. We had so many cones of Alpaca yarn which we had made into skeins and balls. Some of the skeins we had already dyed and they were such beautiful colours. Whilst I knit and crochet, I wanted to be able to make something that was really light in weight and with unique colours.
I was fortunate that the tutor of the Spinning Class, was also the tutor for Weaving. I say 'fortunate' for I already knew that she was a very patient and compassionate person!
She provided a choice of looms to use and also provided all the other equipment needed, including a huge choice of yarns. The first day was fantastic and I was thrilled to be there. The looms were already set up with yarn and all I had to do was take the yarn through the 'shed' (the gap between two lines of yarn). It was just so easy, back and forth only having to change the 'shed' at the end of each row to make a pattern from the instructions provided. I was extremely proud of the very short scarf I made with its lovely pattern and two coloured yarns. Happy days!

The next tuition day though was completely different and this time the tutor started using what to me was a foreign language. We had migrated from the word 'shed' and opened up a completely new vocabulary. Words like 'warp/sett/reed/weft/shaft' entered the training and I had no idea what she was talking about. My brain was stunned and I felt sure I wouldn't be able to do this.

But, that night I sat and read The Big Book of Weaving by Laila Lundell. The help it offered was invaluable and in one reading I was able to not only understand the language, but was able to assimilate all the tutoring I been given that day.

After that, life in class was a breeze. I tried all sorts of yarns and patterns and finished the course with renewed confidence in my abilities.
Of course, armed with the new knowledge, we invested in a loom. There are many different types and sizes and much depends on the size of the space you have, and what sort of things you intend to make. I chose a collapsible table top loom which when folded takes up little room.

The world truly was our oyster after that, with money saved on Christmas presents as family members and friends all got given woven scarves!
Since then we have migrated to bigger and better scarves, wraps, stoles, throws, cushion covers and of course just fabric to cut and make into other things.

It is amazing that all of these things are a result of a fleece that has simply been carded making all the strands go in one direction so that it can be spun.

Carding and Combing

Carding is a process which simply ensures that all the fibre ends up in a parallel state. You can use hand carders for this which look like a dog's brush although a lot larger. The product from hand-carding is called a 'rolag'. Hand-carding though is a long process and made my hands ache, so we eventually moved to a drum carder which means you can card a lot more fleece.

Drum-carders are easily used providing you tease or pick (pull apart) the fleece to start off with. The picking will of course loosen any dirt or organic matter that you didn't pull out prior to storing your fleeces. The more you pick – the more stuff will fall out so make sure you have something for this to fall onto – preferably not your own clothing! No matter how much preparation work you do, you can be sure that the drum-carder will find more dust and organic matter and this falls through a small slot onto your working surface.

If you are using a drum-carder this is a great time to start blending different colours together. You can use the natural colour fibre from your coloured fleeces or the fibre that you have hand dyed. Arranging the fibre in different orders will create different patterns. Do remember that what you see on the drum carder will be different once you have spun it! My drum carder easily provides me with 50gm of fibre – called 'batts'. There are however much bigger drum-carders you can purchase or hire.

Combing is process using steel combs which are extremely sharp – do mind your fingers. Unlike carding, combing removes all short hairs usually caused by second cuts. You end up with two piles of fibre, one contains all the really good fibre (tops or slivers) in a long strand, and the other, fibre that has been combed out which you set aside to use for something else.

Again, with either of these processes you are learning a new language, but you do end up with your fibre processed suitable for spinning.
The book Color in Spinning mentioned before gives a step by step guide on all of these processes.

For the purpose of this book though, whether you have made rolags, batts, tops or slivers (or any other name used in different parts of the world), all are completely saleable. Lots of spinners do not want to have to do the preparatory work and in doing it for them you are providing a really good service and monetising your fleece. The carded or combed fibre is also used for both dry and wet-felting which provides yet another market.

Wet and Dry (Needle) Felting

Felt fabric is a beautiful, tactile fabric that is easy to work with. It can be used for many different things from fun toys, decorations and stylish accessories for the home and to wear. For those of you who have washed a woollen jumper on the wrong temperature, you know how easy it is to felt a garment with overly hot water.

Wet Felting – It is outside the remit of this book to tell you how to felt but suffice it to say wet felting involves, water, soap and lots of elbow grease. The constant agitation of carded fibre laid out in a pattern of your choice provides the much needed felt.

Felt made in this way can be used for a multitude of things. You can mould it into shape for something like a hat, or simply keep it flat to use for making soft toys, decorations, cushion covers, throws etc. or to be cut up for clothing.

Needle Felting – as it implies needle felting is done by constantly piercing your carded fibre (be careful of your fingers) with special barbed needles that interlock the fibres until they bond together. Very useful for embellishing items with decorative motives or jazzing up accessories for the home or clothing. Using a polystyrene base or an armature made from pipe cleaners or metal, you can make the most beautiful toys.

In the book Quick & Clever Felting by Ellen Kharade she shows you how to both wet and dry felt and provides lots of lovely ideas of what to do with your felt. It contains lots of easy to understand instructions. Both methods will add value to your fibre and whatever you produce, and will help recoup the cost of your shearing.

Needle Felting in particular is a great way to use up odds and ends, particular for the bits that form the base of toys.

Toy Making and Stuffing

Toys are very popular items to sell and whether you use your alpaca fibre to knit, crochet, or felt the toy, they will always need stuffing. Whilst in most instances we will be using the blanket (1sts) for our garments and home accessories, when it comes to stuffing we use the 2nd grade. This comes from the neck, rump, legs and belly. In some countries the 2nd grade is further sub-divided so that neck and rump are classed as 2nd and legs and belly are classed as 3rd. As I don't separate these at shearing time, I refer to all of these bits as 2nd grade.

For stuffing you need to have washed and teased (picked) your fibre first. Remember in doing this we are pulling the fibre apart, not only does this remove any organic matter that remains, but it aerates the fibre. If you fail to tease your fibre, you will end up with lumps and bumps in your stuffing rather than a soft squidgy toy.

If you want to use your stuffing for much bigger items like cushions, and quilts then I would recommend using the needle felting technique at spaced intervals to stop the fibre bunching up with use or washing.
Teased too much stuffing? – Just put it out for the birds – they love to build their nests with it.

There are pieces of equipment you can purchase especially for picking. They are really useful if you want to prepare a large amount of fibre. Personally I find it very therapeutic to do it by hand during those long drawn out winter nights. But what if, you don't enjoy any crafts and having understood the need to increase its value, you want someone else to do it for you? Should you get another crafts person to do it for you?

Crafting v Not Crafting

Without any doubt at all if you want a healthy return on your fleeces then you need to either learn a craft or pay someone else to do it for you.

Carding - Yes it does take time but it is worth it. You can sell carded fibre to spinners and felters. You can pay your local Mill to do it for you, but this will increase your own costs which will in turn increase the cost of your product.

Spinning - I found spinning difficult at first but now it's really easy and therapeutic. If you don't want to do it yourself, contact your local Guild who should be able to give you the name of lots of spinners eager to take on your job. Do find out though how much your chosen hand spinner will charge as you will need to factor this in. Having the fleece spun at the Mill increases the cost to you and should be taken into account with your costing.

Knitting and crochet – Whilst I have not touched on this subject, clearly your spun yarn can be used for knitting and crochet. If you are experienced in either of these fields then you will find no difficulty in adapting any pattern to suit the ply of your alpaca yarn. Alternatively, there are many people who enjoy this as a hobby and will take up your offer to make up your yarn into something you have chosen. There are no set rules for what their charges are, so do ask first.

There are a few businesses that are devising patterns for their yarn and selling the pattern with sufficient yarn to make the product. This is yet another monetising option.

Weaving – Once I understood the language, I found weaving really easy. It does take time to set up the loom but after that weaving is really quick, and produces lovely accessories for the home and clothing. It can also be used as cloth. Again, you could find someone to do this for you, or your local Mill may offer this service.

Dyeing – We added lots of choices to our buyers with the introduction of many different colours. I have no idea how much it costs to have this done professionally but certainly my local Mill would not spin fibre after it has been dyed.

Felting – There is so much you can do with felt whether it's wet felt or needle felt. You are spoilt for choice in what you can make.
All of the above will give more value to your fleeces but what if you simply just want to sell the fleece?

Selling Your Fleece - It's up to you whether you sell the blanket on its own or you sell it with the 2nd grade fibre (neck, rump, legs and belly). Either way you need to weigh it so your buyer knows what you are offering. Many Spinning Guilds are happy to purchase your Alpaca Fleeces so that should be your first port of call. They will certainly pay you a lot more than many of the merchants who will buy your fleece and then sell it on.

In many instances, the latter option may not cover your shearing costs. You also have the choice of selling a whole fleece or selling in smaller packages i.e. 50gm, 100gm, 200gm and so on. This is a good way of introducing people to the joy of using Alpaca fleece.

In my case I didn't find a spinner who would buy my fleeces, because a member of the Spinning Guild was also an alpaca breeder and had sold their own fleeces to them. So what's the next option? I had to find other ways to let people know about my fleeces and products.

Chapter 7. How and Where to Sell

How to market your Fleeces and resulting products is a book in itself, but here are some general tips which I hope you will find useful:

Craft Fairs – there are a huge number of these taking place throughout the year. The cost of a stall varies but you can display not only your fleece but all of the resulting products. Take the time to display them nicely so that they look attractive. Put out raw fleeces showing their best attributes. Also list the weights of the fleece. If you have separated the blankets from the 2nds then give the weight of each and of course a price for the blanket and a lower price for the 2nds.

If you have made yarns, make sure you have nice professional looking labels that detail the weight of the yarn and that it is 100% alpaca (provided it is), you should also give the ply of the yarn. These rules apply whether you have made the yarn into balls or skeins (hanks).

Seasonal Fairs/Country Markets – there is a season for almost everything nowadays. Apart from the normal Christmas, New Year, Summer, Winter, Autumn, Spring there is also Mother's Day, Father's Day and all sorts of other 'Days'. There's cricket season, tennis season, golf season, football season and so on. These are all times that you can exploit with products made especially for this occasion.

Your Own Website - If you don't have one, then now is a good time to get one. There are so many free websites now on offer with instructions written in easy to understand English as opposed to technical language.

Social Media – Facebook – Build a Fan Page on Facebook – it costs nothing and you can advertise all of your alpaca things on it for free. If you have a website, then link your Fan Page to your Website.

Social Media – Twitter – LinkedIn etc. – are all good places to advertise your website or Facebook page.

Free and Fee paying sites – EBay, Etsy, Ravelry, Gumtree, Preloved, Amazon, Folksy, Facebook pages for your area, local papers, free ads, the list is endless. But, be aware of any fees that you have to pay for this cost needs to be factored into your pricing.

Auction on EBay – please don't make the mistake that I see many people making on eBay and starting an auction at 99pence. Not everyone will see your fleece and you may receive only a starting bid. Sadly many fleeces are being sold at the starting price of 99pence! After you have paid your EBay and PayPal fees you have very little left and the fleece has been completely devalued. Always start an auction at the lowest price you are willing to accept bearing in mind your shearing costs.

Remember, if you don't give your fleece or products any value, then neither will anyone else.

Commission based selling – approach your local craft, clothes, accessories etc. shops. Many shops are happy to sell on a commission basis. The commission varies some as low as 10% and others as high as 100%. Try to negotiate a good rate – the higher the commission is, the higher priced you goods will be and the least likely to sell. Decide how much you want and the commission is added.

The alpaca business is a very enjoyable one. This is because of the many shows and events that are usually organized by alpaca farmers at both regional and state levels. These shows and events give you an opportunity to travel to so many areas across the country. At such shows, there is usually a lot of entertainment and excitement that makes them unforgettable events. They also provide you with an avenue to meet new friends and network with other businesses.

How many offspring do alpacas have at one time?

Alpaca females deliver one offspring at a time. The young are called "cria." It is very rare for an alpaca to deliver twins and when this does occur, the babies rarely survive.

What is the length of gestation period for alpacas?

Alpaca females carry their offspring for 11.5 months, but this may vary by 30 days or more. Alpaca females are induced ovulators. The act of breeding stimulates their ovulation, which allows breeders to time deliveries for the most favorable seasons of the year.

Why is alpaca fiber considered to be so special?

Alpaca fiber is an extremely fine and rare specialty fiber, exhibiting a quality exceeding that of cashmere. The hollow fiber has superior insulating abilities, and is five times warmer than wool but lightweight and free of the coarse guard hairs seen in llama fiber.

The entire fleece "blanket" removed from an alpaca is suitable for use in the production of garments, and there are at least 22 naturally occurring colors. (The recognized number of colors varies by country.) As an added plus, alpaca does not cause the itching associated with garments made from sheep's wool.

Genetics

Even if genetics isn't one of your prime areas of interest, you should understand enough about the basics in order to make informed choices in your own breeding program. If you are seriously interested in a more extensive study of genetics, read one of the books on this topic listed in the bibliography.

Mendelian Genetics?

Many animals follow the principles of simple Mendelian genetics – where one gene controls one trait; color, for instance. That makes it very easy to predict possible colors from breeding, and to breed for specific characteristics. Unfortunately, with alpacas, it seems very unlikely that it is this simple!

Most of the characteristics in which we are interested are polygenic (influenced by more than one gene). That makes it much more complex to determine the probabilities of the outcome of any given breeding. Nevertheless, there has been some excellent work done by a number of researchers, not the least of who are Wall and Cole in Australia. Their work has been summarized in Mike Safley's book, "Synthesis of a Miracle", and it provides tables showing the predicted outcomes of breedings, compared to a large number of actual births.

Line breeding or inbreeding?

One of the interesting discussions taking place in the alpaca industry at the moment is the wisdom of breeding animals with common ancestors. It is felt so strongly that this is undesirable, that some of the herd management software highlights common animals in suggested breeding pedigrees so that they may be avoided. This is pretty much at odds with the breeding practices of most other animals.

For example, in breeding dogs, most people concentrate on one or two lines that they like, and re-visit those lines throughout the breeding history, to make sure that the traits that they value are present in their offspring. This is known as line breeding. If it gets as close as breeding father to daughter, or son to mother, then it is inbreeding. Inbreeding is usually considered undesirable.

When line breeding is practiced it is common to outcross to unconnected lines every couple of generations, because it can otherwise lead to reduced productivity, and will accentuate less desirable traits as well as those that are valued. Bear in mind that in line breeding and inbreeding, the possibility of undesirable traits being expressed in the offspring is multiplied. So unless you have many alpacas and can afford failed breeding experiments, outcrossing for desirable traits is preferred over line breeding.

We recommend that you spend some time researching at least the basics of genetics, as this will help you to understand which traits are highly heritable. It is important to know how you can best select suitable sires for breeding to your herd.

Selecting Your Foundation Herd

One of the most critical decisions you will make involves selecting your breeding stock. If you learn nothing else from all your alpaca research, learn how to select stock before you spend a single dollar on animal acquisition.

New breeders have a unique opportunity to position themselves at the forefront of the industry by selecting animals that have superior traits. Knowledge of these traits and how to select them is often the difference between success and failure in the alpaca business. For instance most new purchasers start out knowing what breed and what color of animal they want to select but few are considering several, even more important issues:

- What pedigree they would like to have in their purchase?

- To whom is the animal they are buying bred?

- Who will they breed to in the future?

- To whom will the alpaca's offspring be bred?

The answers to the above questions can be even more important than whether or not the alpacas exhibit good fleece and conformation traits. It is important to spend a lot of time educating yourself as to what to look for in breeding stock. Do this by reading (see bibliography), going to seminars and talking to experienced alpaca farmers. Learn as much as you can. Remember you're going to be in the alpaca business for a long time.

Breeding Methodologies

When people start breeding their animals, they tend to develop through three stages. The first is breeding "pretty to pretty", or "phenotypic" breeding. (Phenotypic means the "look" of the animals in question.) This means selecting one of your females, and breeding her to a show ribbon winner or an animal that caught your eye in some other way. Possibly one recommended by your breeder, or by friends. This is probably the least desirable way to go!

You may not have much idea what you are trying to achieve and, without doing any research, you have no idea what characteristics you are going to inherit. This could do lasting damage to your herd. Unfortunately, it is the most common approach to breeding in the USA.

For people that have considered the issue further, the next level is to breed "pedigree to pedigree" or "genotypic" breeding. (Genotypic means breeding for the genes carried by particular lines, regardless of the look of the animals to be bred.) This is much better, because at least you understand what you are trying to achieve, and how to go about it. The problem with this is that you don't know if the herdsire you pick is actually throwing cria that carry the traits in which you are interested.
So, the third and best method with which to pick a herdsire is a development on the second process.

After having identified the male that seems to carry the traits that you want, you then look at the offspring he has produced, to see if they did in fact improve in the desired areas. If the herdsire is doing his job, the crias should be an improvement on their dams. If you can see these improvements, then there is a reasonable chance that he will be able to provide the genes you want for your herd.

Of course, whichever method you adopt, it is essential to check the medical history of both animals, and to see that they are conformationally sound.

Breeding and Birthing

Female alpacas do not have specific "seasons' when they are ready for breeding. They are induced ovulators, meaning that the act of copulation releases the ovum from the follicle. Breedings often are timed in the fall or spring of each year, so that the 11 ½ month gestation period will allow the cria to be born when the weather is comparatively comfortable for them. Farmers that have heated facilities often breed and birth year-round.

Of course, with their origins in the mountains of Peru, where there can be a frost for over 300 days a year, they are not really affected by the winter cold in most of North America. Nevertheless, most people have cria coats available to protect the babies from the worst of the cold weather.

Alpacas usually have just one cria (twins occur about 1 in 2,000 births), weighing around 16 to 22 lbs. They will be weaned at about 6 months of age. The mother can then be rebred 14-21 days after the birth.

Breeding Methods

There are two main methods of breeding alpacas. One is to allow the males to mix with the open females in the paddock, with mating taking place naturally. This has been the traditional way in South America for thousands of years and is often called pasture breeding. The other way, more common in the USA, is pen, or hand, breeding. Here the male is introduced to one female at a time, and the mating is observed to make sure that it happened, and that there were no apparent problems. In order to be able to track the pregnancy accurately, we recommend pen breeding.

Confirmation of pregnancy

After the breeding, hormonal changes in the female influence their behavior toward a male. If a male approaches a pregnant female she will spit him off. This habit is useful for testing for pregnancy. About ten days after breeding, a male is introduced to the female in the field. If she is pregnant, she will spit him off, if she isn't she will allow another breeding. This practice is known as "tease testing", and it is usual to do this for the first month.

After about 30 days, a progesterone or ultrasound test is performed to confirm the pregnancy. This may be repeated at around 90 days, with periodic tease testing in between.

Birthing

Well before the estimated birth date, you need to prepare for the new cria. This includes getting all the equipment you will need for both normal and emergency births. Below is a list of suggested items to have on hand:

Item	What it may be needed for
Birthing Kit - General	
Birthing – Observation Log sheets	Record times and observations
Timing Clock	Time labor
Neonatal Care book and other reference material	Reference
Cell Phone	Call for Help!
Trash bags	For disposing of placenta and for usual purposes
Birthing Kit – Dam Supplies	
Iodine scrub soap (e.g. Betadine Scrub)	To clean perineum (genital area)
4 x 4 gauze pads	To clean perineum (genital area)
Lubricating gel – water based such as K-Y Jelly, large amount. (do not use a petroleum based lubricant like Vaseline)	To be used if performing internal exam or adjustment
Disposable plastic gloves (long sleeved)	To be used if performing internal exam or adjustment
Vet wrap or similar cling material	To wrap the tail
Forceps Clamp	To hold and clip the tail to the back – out of the way for exam.
Domperidone (2 tubes)	If no milk, give mother 5cc orally BID x 5 days
Oxytocin, 1L Sterile NS, IV set, 100cc PCN	Uterine Lavage
Birthing Kit – Cria Supplies	
Towels/blankets	Drying the cria
0.5% chlorhexidine (*Nolvasan*), preferred over iodine	To treat cria's umbilical cord

Item	What it may be for
35mm film canister or similar small container	To hold the iodine again: cria's belly
Small wide mouth jar with heavy string soaked in iodine or Navel clamp	To tie off or clamp off u1 cord
Bulb syringe (nasal aspirator)	May be needed to clear a
Stomach tube & feeding syringe	In case Cria is unable to
Empty Pediatric Enema Bottle - for 2 ounce warm water enema.	In case cria does not def€ normally within 24 hrs.
Bo-Se (1 mg/ml selenium and 50 mg/ml Vit E) & syringe (Note: do not use Mu-Se)	Only in areas that are sel deficient.
Vitamin supplement (vit D or E)	Appears in some referen€ but not all.
Hand-held hair dryer	To dry off or to warm th€
Frozen goat or cow colostrum	In case cria needs colostı
Frozen Plasma	If no colostrums is avail
Cria coat	In case baby gets a chill.
Lamb nipples and plastic bottle	In case you have to feed
Foal nasogastric tubes	
Blood sample kit	To draw blood to test IgC
Mineral oil fleet enema	For premature or weak cı at 8-12 hrs. and 18-24 hr:

Most births occur during the daylight hours, often in the morning. It is suggested that this is an inherited trait; necessary in their native Andes. Alpacas born during the hours of darkness would be in danger from predators, and the cria would have to be able to walk with the herd by early evening when they moved to a new grazing area.

Alpacas tend to give birth easily, without needing intervention. This is probably true in 90% of the cases. For the remainder, it is necessary to know when to step in to help. Birthing problems can include mispresentation (dystocia), failure to nurse, "wall babies", premature crias cleft palate (choanal atresia), and hypothermia. There are excellent books on neonatal care that will help you to understand the implications and actions needed in these cases (see bibliography).

Also highly recommended is participation in one the several neonatal seminars that are presented around the country. These seminars provide excellent hands-on training by modeling difficult birthing situations.

The stages

There are three main stages in the birthing process:

Stage One – Contractions, frequent visits to the dung pile, possibly accompanied by restlessness. (Although some alpacas show virtually no signs prior to birth.)

Stage Two – Begins about 30 minutes before the birth, when the cria enters the birth canal. The cria should present head and front feet first. The feet should burst the bag. If they don't you should break it yourself when the head is visible, to avoid the possibility of the baby drowning.

Most alpacas deliver standing up, but some do it while cushing. It is common for the mother to walk about with the baby hanging out for a few minutes. This is not a problem, unless it continues for too long.

Stage Three – The expulsion of the placenta. This usually happens about 45 minutes after the birth, but it could take a few hours.

Hopefully, all will go well with your alpaca births but you should be prepared. Read up on the subject, so that you know how long to wait before calling the vet, what danger signs you should look for, as well as having all the necessary supplies on hand. For the first birth at least, your breeder should be available either in person or by telephone, to give you support and advice.

As with most other things in life, you will get out of it what you put in. If you are prepared to work hard at marketing your farm, and are comfortable talking to people and selling to them, you can make a very comfortable living with alpacas.

Conclusion

If you start with an investment of (£80000) $100,000, plan your business properly, manage it effectively, and sell your animals and products successfully, you could easily generate an income of over (£120000) $150,000 a year after 4 years.

There are a number of ways you can take part in an alpaca business, ranging from a straightforward financial investment, to a full farming business. You can also add in peripheral activities such as fiber wholesaling, processing, and the sale of spinning products.

Whichever path you decide to follow I am sure you will find that, like most people in the business, it will turn out to be a rewarding and life-changing experience

Made in the USA
Las Vegas, NV
31 July 2022